Promiscuous

Portnoy's Complaint and Our
Doomed Pursuit of Happiness

Bernard Avishai

Yale UNIVERSITY PRESS   NEW HAVEN & LONDON

Published with assistance from the foundation established in memory of Philip Hamilton McMillan of the Class of 1894, Yale College.

Yale University Press books may be purchased in quantity for educational, business, or promotional use. For information, please e-mail sales.press@yale.edu (U.S. office) or sales@yaleup.co.uk (U.K. office).

Set in Janson type by Integrated Publishing Solutions.
Printed in the United States of America.

Library of Congress Cataloging-in-Publication Data
Avishai, Bernard.
Promiscuous : *Portnoy's Complaint* and our doomed pursuit of happiness / Bernard Avishai.
p.   cm.
Includes bibliographical references and index.
ISBN 978-0-300-15190-9 (alk. paper)
1. Roth, Philip. Portnoy's complaint.   2. Satire, American—History and criticism.   3. Jews in literature.   I. Title.   II. Title: Portnoy's complaint and our doomed pursuit of happiness.
PS3568.O855P6733   2012
813'.54—dc22   2011040563

A catalogue record for this book is available from the British Library.

This paper meets the requirements of ANSI/NISO Z39.48–1992 (Permanence of Paper).

10 9 8 7 6 5 4 3 2 1

For Maya, Sofia, Lina, and Jorie, our little monkeys

. . . the artist descends within himself, and in that lonely region of stress and strife, if he is deserving and fortunate, he finds the terms of his appeal. His appeal is made to our less obvious capacities: to that part of our nature which, because of the warlike conditions of existence, is necessarily kept out of sight within the more resisting and hard qualities—like the vulnerable body within a steel armor. His appeal is less loud, more profound, less distinct, more stirring—and sooner forgotten. Yet its effect endures forever.

—Joseph Conrad, from his introduction to *The Nigger of the "Narcissus,"* as quoted to his literature class by the writer Nathan Zuckerman, as depicted in his story "Courting Disaster" by the writer Peter Tarnopol, from the novel *My Life as a Man* by Philip Roth, 1974

Contents

Contents

Teaching Notes

Most people I have asked remember where they were when they read *Portnoy's Complaint,* something like when President Kennedy was shot—a more cheerful memory, needless to say, but one that sticks for much the same reason. Reading Philip Roth's yellow-clad book felt like the end of innocence, which (for Boomers, curiously) had a way of ending again and again. Or was it that we felt unexpectedly discovered?

Who in the history of the world has been least able to deal with a woman's tears? My father. I am second. He says to me, "You heard your mother. Don't eat French fries with Melvin Weiner after school."

"Or ever," she pleads.

"Or ever," my father says.

"Or hamburgers out," she pleads.

"Or hamburgers out," he says.

"*Hamburgers*," she says bitterly, just as she might say *Hitler*, "where they can put anything in the world in that they want—and *he* eats them. Jack, make him promise, before he gives himself a terrible *tsura*, and it's too late.

"I *promise!*" I scream. "I *promise!*" and race from the kitchen—to where? Where else.

I tear off my pants, furiously I grab that battered battering ram to freedom, my adolescent cock, even as my mother begins to call from the other side of the bathroom door. "Now this time don't flush. Do you hear me, Alex? I have to see what's in that bowl!"

Doctor, do you understand what I was up against? My wang was all I really had that I could call my own . . .

The first I heard of the book, a friend from McGill immediately began reading me long passages on the phone. I knew students who sat around in coffee shops, student unions, and Hillel houses reading the entire book out loud to one another, a kind of spontaneous, burlesque Bloomsday. A lawyer friend in Boston wrote: "One reason I married Joni was because when she and I first met, we coincidentally were both reading *Portnoy's Complaint*, found it uproarious, and I knew we were right for each other."

Yet Roth found—how does Conrad put it?—"the terms of his appeal" not only among people now over sixty, and not only among American Jews. By 1975, six years after the book's publication, *Portnoy's Complaint* had sold nearly half a million copies in hardback in the United States, three and a half million in paperback.[1] The novel was then translated into virtually every language where you did not have to explain the term "neurotic," including Finnish, Hungarian, and Japanese. American librarians still consistently list *Portnoy's Complaint* among the twentieth century's top one hundred.[2] Search it on Google and you get well over 85,000 hits. By contrast, Zadie Smith's breakout novel, *White Teeth*, which was published in 2000, gets about 78,000. Amazon has more than 110 reader reviews of *Portnoy's Complaint*, which now outsells *The Great Gatsby*. The librarians' favorite Web site, "The Library Thing," has over 60 reviews (some no longer than passionate blog posts) dealing with the book as if it had been published last week. One thoughtful reader, who signed on as George D. Ross, put it this way: "Disturbing and discomfiting at times . . . but even after all this time, it's amazing how fresh and surprising Portnoy's voice is, how brutally honest his analysis of family life. I'm still trying to make sense of the fact that this was once a nationwide bestseller . . ."

We remember Alex Portnoy impaling with pitiless thrusts invasive mothers, plugged-up fathers, dizzying women in heat. We remember, with sympathetic relief, Portnoy's letting go with an utter version of himself, the way we could only imagine someone erupting on the analyst's couch, as if back then we *could* really imagine, let alone afford, the analyst's couch. Portnoy spoke of pleasuring himself hungrily, though pleasure hardly seemed the word for it. Let's get this out of the way: you still can get intelligent, graying people to laugh out loud simply by coupling "Alex" with "liver." For the brothers among us, who did not share Portnoy's belief that standing under a fly ball, *knowing you would make the catch*, could turn center field into a delusionary metaphor for "life"? As for sisters, who was not thrilled to find confirmation for the sheer power of panties? (Then again, I recently visited a midwestern campus where I was instructed by a young professor of Women's Studies that Portnoy's lust—actually, "Roth's misogyny"—is now studied only with the precautions one takes examining any other biological hazard.)

And Portnoy took on—or, more accurately, refused to let off—his American Jewish family. This was immediately assumed to mean Jews in general, which in 1969 seemed especially brazen. It was only twenty-seven years after

1942 and twenty-one years after 1948. American Jews thought they had earned a kind of moral intermission that Portnoy seemed not to be respecting. It was also just two years after the 1967 war, which had made Diaspora Jews and organized American Zionists inarguably (now, unimaginably) cool. Portnoy's tribal wordplay suggested, prophetically, that if Jews had power and bodies, this only meant they'd be struggling with the world-historical sinfulness they had customarily projected onto Gentiles. You put the Id back in Yid, Portnoy instructed, and you come to understand the "oy" in goy.

Portnoy, in other words, spoke so frankly about our arousing parts and sly transgressions—things even Leopold and Molly Bloom mostly insinuated—that it was hard not to feel a kind of shameless release. An elderly Irishman, a retired professor of history, told me recently, "I could not believe what I was reading when I read *Portnoy's Complaint*. I never thought that I could see such things become *literature*." We recall Portnoy avidly moving from one exhausted insight to the next, one exhausted fantasy to the next, punch line to punch line, nipple to nipple—brilliant, aggrieved, promiscuous.

Still, the effect that endures from the art, if not "forever" as Conrad prays, then for much of the past forty years, has been something of a blur. People remember in flashes characters and vignettes like the one I just retrieved. But few can remember the book's architecture or identify any big ideas. Trying to remember the plot is like trying to remember the composition of a Jackson Pollock canvas. The book doesn't really have a hero, so how to account for its champions? Irving Howe wrote back in 1972 that "the cruelest thing anyone can do with *Portnoy's Complaint* is to read it twice."[3] But why would anyone have *needed* to read it twice? For most of us, the moment of reading was what was valuable, then and since, and not simply in the nostalgic sense. "I don't remember much except that Portnoy was funny and bad and vigorous, and that seemed a comfort," a cousin wrote me. That's pretty much how most of us felt. (Howe would eventually change his mind about *Portnoy's Complaint*, by the way. He told me some years later, in the code of the New York intellectuals, that he had underestimated Roth's "great talent for dialogue.")

This is all puzzling. How could the experience of reading a book evoke such vivid appreciation and leave such a fuzzy imprint? Conrad supposed that great art necessarily grows "less distinct" over the years. Yet *Heart of Darkness* had, as they say, a takeaway. What was the takeaway from *Portnoy's Complaint*? Did it have an implication that explains, at least in part, why it traveled through generations of readers? Just last year, in a zany bit about holy books at the time of the Ground Zero mosque controversy, *The*

Daily Show's Jon Stewart pulled out *Portnoy's Complaint* as the American Jewish text to go up against the Koran and the New Testament. You might think: a ribald book with a cult following among funny Jews (again, you heard a lot about sexual assaults on the family dinner). Yet Garrison Keillor once introduced Roth as "the author of America's greatest satire." Really? Alex Portnoy, the quintessential American anything?

Anyway, the mission of this, my own little book, is to make Roth's novel more distinct. The clock is ticking on him and on us. If we consider why *Portnoy's Complaint* has endured in its way we might well learn something interesting about Roth, ourselves, the uses of fiction, and the country that's made room for us since its publication. We might even learn something about Conrad's "warlike conditions of existence," about which Portnoy was, in *his* way, something of an aficionado.

Roth has had time and reason to reflect on these questions himself. He was for most of his career a teacher of literature, and the reception of the book fascinated him as a critic, even as it changed his life. It became a subject to work on in later novels, *My Life as a Man, Zuckerman Unbound, The Ghost Writer,* and others. He and I have spoken many times, in little exchanges, about *Portnoy's Complaint* since we first got to know each other back in

1974—particularly since the early 1980s, as talk deepened into banter and teasing and friendly counsel. Portnoy's insatiable, lampooning voice has never been very far beneath the surface of our talk; any moment of gloom would be helpless against its timing. (*Bernard! What are you doing in there!*)

Perhaps the most considered statement Roth made about his book was in teaching notes he prepared for a class on his work at Bard College in the fall of 1999. The class was taught by Roth's friend the writer Norman Manea, a member of the Bard faculty. Manea taught a novel of Roth's one day—not only *Portnoy's Complaint*, but also *The Counterlife*, *American Pastoral*, and *I Married a Communist*—and Roth drove down the next from his home in Connecticut to meet Manea's students and share his own perspective on the work in question. When I undertook to write this book, and needed to jump-start my own thinking, Roth and I spoke at length, though informally, about the timing and themes of the novel. He also shared his teaching notes with me. They begin as follows:

A polemic mood.

One is under no constraints with satire.

The grotesque conception of his life and the lives
     around him is what is being dramatized.

Flies in the face of the normalizing passion.

Caricature? Of course. He holds a grotesque conception of his life and this creates the coarseness of the
realism. To criticize R. for not being "balanced" is
like criticizing Moliere for not being "fair."
Lets the grotesque into *the satiric conception of a Jewish
family*, the son *included*. The greatest object of the
satire is the narrating Portnoy!

Two things jump out at you and they seem of a piece.
The first is Roth's depiction of Portnoy's narrative—his
character's grasp of his recounted life—as "grotesque."
This implies a skepticism about Portnoy, and a serious-
ness of purpose in his creator, that one might not have
supposed given how clever Portnoy seems and how hard
he's made us laugh. I mean, Portnoy had such a mouth on
him. He seemed so textured, so open, so often on the
money, that young readers especially could hardly avoid
identifying with him. In his early stories, collected in
Goodbye, Columbus, Roth had proven the menace of his
wit. And he admits later in his teaching notes that he was
astounded that he had had the nerve to write the book
thirty years earlier. "On rereading what I wrote in my
early thirties," he writes, "I'm shocked and pleased:
shocked that I could have been so reckless; pleased that
I should have been so reckless." Didn't "the narrating
Portnoy" simply take the author's own voice to a new

level of astringency and allow him to say things with "no constraint"?

No, it did not. "The greatest object of the satire is the narrating Portnoy!" Roth insists in his notes; a novel in the form of a confession is for God's sake not a confession in the form of a novel. Roth has stressed the distinction virtually from the time of *Portnoy's Complaint*'s publication and *still* felt the need to instruct his Bard students (most of them probably clueless about why he was bothering to tell them this at all) that the author's "balance" was not the point when he invented Portnoy, no more than Molière's "fairness."

"I was trying to break from my literary conscience," Roth continues, "as it has been constructed by my reading, my teachers, even my fears. The background *I* was overthrowing was literary." He was determined to "let the repellent in":

Masturbation, which seems to have made the book famous, was the least of it. It was the aggressive rage, the ingratitude, the hatred that was the most shameful secret.

The notes continue:

One is not here as a writer, or as an artist of any kind, to be loved. This is hard to accept, even for a writer. But that's the sad truth.

I had published three responsible books. Responsible to what? Was not looking for my catharsis as patient, a neurotic, a son. Looking, as one perpetually looks, for my freedom as a writer.

Portnoy was a concoction, you see, a way of exploring the *Drang* before the *Sturm* in a young man's life. Portnoy's lewdness, rage, ingratitude, et cetera, were just a small part of what was wrong with him. Nor, Roth supposed, was making all of this seem natural going to win the author many friends. Portnoy was going to be "the man who is the repository of every socially unacceptable thought," all the more unacceptable for lacking dignity: "They're not even *dignified* complaints," the notes go on; "They aren't the *dignified* unacceptable thoughts. They are really the stinky unacceptable thoughts."

Which brings me to the second thing, the phrase "flies in face of the normalizing passion." Roth does not write "flies in face of the normal," which you'd expect from a satire; he writes of the zeal for the normal, which leaves you wondering. The satirist is under "no constraints," at least insofar as he or she may employ (here comes the *OED*) "humor, irony, exaggeration, or ridicule to expose and criticize people's stupidity or vices, particularly in the context of contemporary politics and other topical issues." But satirists are usually constrained in a way Roth elides here. They amuse readers by assuming a desired moral principle, a norm, that's so obviously at odds with some social convention or human foible that satire can ridicule, through humor, irony, and so on, people who fall short. Okay, the impulse to conform can itself be amusing. (The hero in Monty Python's *Life of Brian*, suddenly presumed the messiah, tries to disown his adoring followers: "You are all individuals!" he shouts—to which the crowd answers as one, "Yes, we are all individuals!" One solitary voice pipes up: "*I'm* not!") But the urge to normalize cannot mean *only* this fretful kind of conformism. Every satire, like every sentence in a way, is a tribute to the presumption that words aim to set standards—the good to which all things aim, as Aristotle famously put it. I don't mean to get too pedantic here, but the normalizing passion suggests an ethical, not just a psychological, impulse. Satirists from Jonathan Swift to George Carlin implicitly projected a *new* normal. If they did not, how could they shame public figures, or readers, for that matter, into improvement?

I may be getting a little ahead of myself, but Roth seems to be signaling something intriguing, if not unique, about the book's hero: a voice that gives us no clue to the normal because it can never seem to impeach other voices without impeaching its own as well ("'I haven't gained five pounds,' she says, 'since you were born. Feel,' she says, and holds my stiff fingers against the swell of her hips, which aren't bad . . ."). The book, Roth goes on, is distinctive for its apparent "improvisational chaos," which mirrors Portnoy's mania, his unwillingness to be "constrained by his moral conscience": "One is not here as a writer, or as an artist of any kind, to be loved."

Yet for all of Roth's protestations, I bet most of those Bard students, like countless readers before them, *have* loved Roth for this book. They could not assume Portnoy's story was simply grotesque. They could not assume Portnoy's voice was, first and foremost, self-satirizing. Portnoy remained adorable somehow, the consummate stand-up comic, his parents and lovers the justified targets of his petulance, the character through which Roth liberated his voice and his spirit. It has been hard to see Roth's protagonist as a mere literary device. It still is, harder than ever, maybe. *Now vee may perhaps to begin. Yes?*

Let me not beat around the bush. I want to show that, sure, Roth's great book gave "the narrating Portnoy" scope to rail against what was comic, even grotesque, in families—Jewish families, WASP families, *immigrant* families. We laughed and mocked and blushed. And the sex— ah, the *talk* of sex—was right there, first alone in the bathroom, then with Portnoy's immortal dreamboat, The Monkey ("*Did I eat!*"), and finally in a wave of impotence in a Tel Aviv hotel. The writer Nelson Aldrich remembers the "refreshing relief" of being able to think about masturbation especially as a form of cultural insurgency. "There was also the hard, disturbing word 'cunt,' which is still disturbing," another friend added. And *Portnoy's Complaint* had other firsts, at least for my generation: riffs on pompous clergy, too-righteous-by-half liberals, too-smug-by-three-quarters Israelis. None of these explain the book's iconic status as the sixties' most iconoclastic work.

Rather, much as Roth implied, *Portnoy's Complaint* gave readers an enigma that has lodged in the back of our minds along with the caricature, something to do with a voice that cannot mock others without first mocking itself, something enduring because it was so disorienting. This was the sound of a psychoanalytic room, yet there was no way to judge or sympathize with what we were hearing—no vantage point, no moral pivot, nothing but an eavesdropping on analysand and analyst, both of whom seemed verging on parody. Roth presumed an audience familiar with the rhythms of the psychoanalytic project, or half-mischievously, half-presumed it. The rhetorical gambit is what made satire of "the normalizing passion" even conceivable.

Roth picks up this point himself in the teaching notes:

Psychoanalysis provided the vessel for everything. In psychoanal. nothing is too petty, nothing is too grand.

The place where you're allowed to say anything.
Allows for hatred, aggression, pettiness; *nothing
censored.* If that's the bargain, that's the bargain.
Coarse realism. Any type of exaggeration is permissible. *It* takes the liberties for you.

Roth was determined (so he adds) to take Freud's dark
wisdom "as seriously as possible"—to see family relations
as dramatic, not only as primary experience, but because
they were set off against the backdrop of Freud's mythic
theories of evolving personality. Constraints were *necessarily* gone, not only because satire invited it, but therapy
demanded it. So Portnoy's madness seemed true without
purporting to make the book's readers sane.

Harold Bloom writes that *Portnoy's Complaint* left readers pulling for a character whose ambition and self-subversion could never be told apart; that Roth forced us
to feel ourselves in a state of anxious futility with Portnoy,
like the proverbial Jew who is told: "Sleep faster, we need
the pillows."[4] And the Jewish home was just the right
place to find such a character, a place where the superego
had gained a five-thousand-year head start. This hardly
made Roth a Jewish writer. It made Jews useful to an
American tragedian. ("Jews are members of the human
race," Roth penned onto his typed notes; "worse than that
I cannot say about them.") Portnoy's push into America

was archetypal: relentless, carnal, and doomed. Every journey of ambition was bound to blow up in its own fuel. The synagogue bulletin suggested, too, stories worthy of Sherwood Anderson; a few weeks with The Monkey could leave even a lascivious Jew as restless as Gatsby himself.

One might conclude that the hero of the novel must then be the forbearing Dr. Spielvogel. Certainly, it was hard to hear all the *kvetching* and not sense what Spielvogel must have been thinking, that freedom was not (or not only) complaint, that narcissism could become what Christopher Lasch would call "a culture." Alas, the enigma of *Portnoy's Complaint* is bigger yet. For the novel leaves us with the lingering suspicion that the analyst, too, was a little too prone to extreme inventions; that he represented an orthodoxy that thought it had an explanation for everything, from pleasure to process—that psychoanalysis took "liberties" for Spielvogel, too.

Not coincidentally—so Roth finished his class—every normalizing passion had a way of turning orthodox and thus quite possibly vicious. The key moment in the book, he said, is when Uncle Hymie beats up Cousin Heshie just for entertaining the idea of marrying a *shikse*—a show of brutality in the most conventional sense:

> The truly repellent, but not on the Dost. scale. Not murder. Not Genet—not theft and sodomy. No, the

truly repellent at the local domestic level. That which is brutal and is everywhere.

That which is brutal and everywhere. Did *Portnoy's Complaint*, in shaming such brutality, wind up defending the biggest norm of them all, or at least the most Yankee: that we must question everything, taking our liberties where we cannot justify denying them? Is the narrating Portnoy America's classical fool, his vulgarity bringing us to our senses?

I confess, as if we need more confessions, that I undertake this writing feeling a bit of a fool myself. You have to be as fresh, or vain, as Portnoy to think you could write about *Portnoy's Complaint*. Readers like books about books about as much as they like a cousin's snapshots of Prague. And they have been on particularly intimate terms with *this* book. *Portnoy's Complaint* is about everything that matters, which is to say everything that hurts. You want rapture? There is rapture. You want meaning? Portnoy is a sucker for rapture *as* meaning, though his most solid experience of it is a hard-on with a farcically short half-life. The book is ostensibly about Portnoy's perverse desire in particular. But once it has done its work, what more is there to say about desire in general? And *Portnoy's Complaint* evokes our most daunting time of life. Dickens lives on because he speaks to the bullied, ambitious child in us. Salinger speaks to a teenager's rejection of phonies. Roth, in contrast, speaks to and through the nervous young person who lives on in us more resiliently; speaks to that hyper-precious moment when the child goes into eclipse, the teen having long before been launched, and adult pleasures (bodies, risk, power) and their surprising allies (dissembling, aggression, moral equivocation) present themselves.

Write about *Portnoy's Complaint* and you will inevitably be seen as judging the whole oeuvre of a writer whom virtually every reader has an opinion about—sort of the way people who say they know nothing about business have opinions about the car business. Even if readers of the novel could be persuaded that Portnoy is nothing like Roth, they'll think they *know* Roth, and in certain important ways they do. Conclusions about this, his most famous work, suggest a personality, a *presence*—something far more intimate than a life story. My book is not a biography of Roth, I hasten to add. If anything, it aims to leave readers doubting that there could ever be a problem for which a biography is the solution. Imagine that a biographer revealed how Roth had had an affair in this or that year, or had episodes of melancholy here or there. Who, after reading *Portnoy's Complaint*, let alone Roth's thirty other works of fiction, would find this intriguing?

Should we trust anyone but Roth to tell us what we need to know of his love, ambitions, and madness—do we not read him to understand how to *define* love, ambitions, and madness? Aldrich once told me that he credits Roth with writing a new book anticipating "every new phase of life, just before I was about to experience it." (With *Everyman*, we even get a phase called dying.)

Portnoy's Complaint, in short, was a prodigy's most sensational fiction, not coincidentally about a prodigiously articulate protagonist. One cannot write about either without presumption. Almost everybody who admires Roth's calmest voice has a vaguely protective attitude toward Portnoy's manic one. Many have imagined themselves closest to Shakespeare by drawing close to Hamlet, who was smart about himself up to a point. We imagine ourselves closest to Roth through Portnoy, who is smart about himself up to something like the same point—where knowing you are crazed is no escape from being responsible. Again, being a friend of Roth's does not save one from mixing up the voices at times, or resenting people who, mistaking Portnoy's voice for Roth's, confound his reputation. Roth is no help to his friends here, since he'll spontaneously mix voices up himself, yanking in versions of great American stereotypes one after another: crotchety Jew, Italian punk, academic feminist—and leering Portnoy. It is hard, as I write about the novel, and various conversations come to mind, to remember where Portnoy's shtick leaves off and my hunger for his shtick begins. (*I met a forty-year-old there. I have a sixty-year-old and I still have a thirty-year-old. So I am only missing a fifty-year-old. Do you know where I can get a fifty-year-old?*)

There are other reasons for me to leave this novel alone. It is frighteningly erudite. I am trained in political economy, not literature, and Roth is the only author other than Karl Marx whose every published word I have read. *Portnoy's Complaint* has the energy of willfulness, which Nietzsche warned (a little erudition of my own, ha-ha) can be appreciated only by the pitiless, which I am not. There is a grandeur to Portnoy's promiscuity which I'm not sure a writer in his sixties can revisit without driving himself a little nuts. The novel may now also seem dated—afflicted with an "oddly period feel," as Michael Chabon wrote me—for it pushed an envelope whose sides, thanks inter alia to the novel itself, we no longer feel pressing in on us very much—well, certainly not as in 1969.

Which raises the last danger I can think of in writing about *Portnoy's Complaint*, something like the problem of going meta on the laughter prompted by now hackneyed epithets like "shikses" and "WASPs"—the problem some other writer will no doubt face in 2048, long after CNN talking heads have disappeared, trying to explain how *The*

Daily Show itself achieved iconic status. *Portnoy's Complaint* is, or was, hilarious. If I don't explain the experiences out of which it was wrought—*gestalt*-inducing phrases like "the new Nixon"—younger people will not fully appreciate the joke. If I *do* explain things, I'll ruin the joke. Iconic works have a way of captivating future generations, but also of making themselves seem deceptively tame to future generations.

Anyway, my book assumes a problem: why *Portnoy's Complaint* became so popular, why it remains so important to people, how it came to carry a weight of emotion and insight evoking an "age," how its roster of personalities came to stand for categories, what ethics it implies—why it *bugs* us. The book presents us with unfinished business. My chapters assume the progression of the argument I have been sketching out so far:

In Chapter One, I try to locate *Portnoy's Complaint* in its time: the launch, the confusion of Portnoy's voice with Roth's, the reasons why, given Roth's rhetorical genius, the book has worn so well. Chapter Two follows up the point, looking at Portnoy as satirist, one who shows us through his comedic contradictions what we had felt more poignantly as tragedy, that endless erotic energy fuels bourgeois liberties, that these nervous sensations can wreck any cultivated *jardin*—that tuned-in and turned-on is eventually fucked-up. In Chapter Three, I show how Portnoy's Jewishness not only reinforces his satire of bourgeois limitations, but also makes Portnoy an object of satire, especially to himself; how Roth's Jewish critics missed this point almost entirely. Chapter Four raises the question of whether Roth was giving us a satire through psychoanalysis, or a satire *of* psychoanalysis. I will show that Portnoy is playing to his analyst's peculiar expectations, switching the places of the totem and the taboo; that the analyst, in turn, has a peculiar, fixed response to his patient, which leaves us doubting that any voice here can be trusted.

What is to be made of a satire whose target slides under our hands—from family and lover, to analysand, to analyst—and so seems to keep us sliding on? My Conclusion will wrestle briefly with the novel's instructive ambiguity. "A wonderful fact to reflect upon," Dickens writes, famously, in *A Tale of Two Cities*, "that every human creature is constituted to be that profound secret and mystery to every other." *Portnoy's Complaint* shows us as few books have how we rely on our capacity to invent fictions about one another to establish our singularity and strive against its loneliness.

Roth told PBS interviewer Jeffrey Brown in 2004 that the only cause he was ever "advancing" was the cause of literature—"one of the great lost human causes," which

America may not be bothering with in the foreseeable future. You "do your bit for fiction," which "doesn't get you any less stupid as you age."[5]

There is a kind of faith here, in "doing your bit," though I am not revealing anything not obvious when I say Roth's attitude toward religious sentimentality is not kind. *Redemption? Isn't that when you bring green stamps to the supermarket?* Still, Portnoy reveals a mysterious courage in his complaining and Roth knows it. Portnoy's mix of disappointment, ambition, rage, and recalcitrant desire has "repetition compulsion" written all over it, yet he keeps going. For our part, the readers of *Portnoy's Complaint*, we read with a courage of our own. We want, and *want!* and WANT, things to be different for us.

CHAPTER ONE

A Novel in the Form of a Confession
The Enigma of Portnoy, Who Is Not Roth

By the beginning of 1969, much of *Portnoy's Complaint* had already appeared in print. Excerpts had been published in *Partisan Review* (whose 5,000 bookish copies were passed from hand to hand), *Esquire*, and *New American Review*, the now defunct magazine edited by Roth's friend and early promoter Ted Solotaroff. Rumors about publication rights began to circulate, creating the feeling of an impending literary squall. Random House, which paid Roth a $250,000 advance (about $2.5 million in today's money), published the hardback in February; Bantam paid $350,000 for the paperback rights. ("I wondered," Roth told a friend at the time, "what did you tip the courier who just handed you a check for a quarter of a million dollars?") *Portnoy's Complaint* sold 420,000 copies during the first ten weeks of its going on sale. Over 275,000 sold within two days of the publication date.[1]

At launch, George Plimpton—another early supporter of Roth's work at the *Paris Review*, who was then at the height of his own fame—interviewed Roth for the *New York Times Book Review*. "But surely you don't intend us to believe," Plimpton pressed him, "that this volatile novel of sexual confession, among other things, had its conception in purely literary motives?" Roth answered, not without that tincture of defensiveness that would seep into a hundred future interviews: "[Portnoy] is obscene because he wants to be saved. . . . [His] pains arise out of his refusal to be bound any longer by taboos which, rightly or wrongly, he experiences as diminishing and unmanning. The joke on Portnoy is that for him breaking the taboo turns out to be as unmanning in the end as honoring it. Some joke."[2]

The joke *on* Portnoy? Come on, the jokes were *by* Portnoy. Was the thirty-six-year-old Roth, who had never had a novel sell more than 25,000 copies in hardcover, ducking the blowback from his wicked, perfect aim? Nor did it take more than a few months for *Portnoy's Complaint* to slip into America's cultural currents like a little anchor. Reviewing the book in the *New York Times*, Josh Greenfeld proclaimed that "Portnoy's past comes off as a kind of universal pop boyhood of the forties," albeit "with a Jewish accent and comic twist." We—and again, I don't just mean American Jews—began to refer to its characters, or should I say its targets, as if using a kind of shorthand: Sophie (especially Sophie), The Monkey, "my father," Rabbi Warshaw, Cousin Heshie, Dr. Spielvogel. The main characters became instant archetypes, which younger readers particularly gained a feel for, or had an opinion about, or thought they should have; characters personifying new (or newly admitted) emotions, standards, disturbances—characters on the way to becoming *Jeopardy!* questions. Patches of Portnoy's Jewish-mother-admonitions even entered into our household squabbles. "I know it's a fault, Alex, but I'm too good!" my son, then a teenager, once threw back at me.

Nelson Aldrich, another erstwhile *Paris Review* acquaintance, still thinks of *Portnoy's Complaint* as one of those books "around which you pivoted," and he never thought to ask—so he told me—"What am I doing reading a book from *this quarter?*" Not long ago, *Time* critic Richard Lacayo, rating his all-time favorite novels, recalled the book as "a literary instance of shock and awe."[3] President Obama, greeting the winners of the National Humanities Medal in 2010, Roth among them, asked his audience, "How many young people have learned to think by reading the exploits of Portnoy and his complaints?" (Roth told me that as Obama actually presented the medal, he whispered, "You're not slowing down, are you?" Roth had to disappoint him by admitting that he was.) So the reaction to the novel was immediate, and the legend of Portnoy's strikes kept building. The novel was cited in journals and academic literature even more often in the 1990s than in the 1970s.[4]

You have to start with the sex, or what passed for sex when you were young in midcentury. At least since Augustine's *Confessions*, there have been readers drawn to coming-of-age stories with sexual hunger driving the plot and moral torment prompting Help. You have to wonder, as I have reason to suspect its author does, if *Portnoy's Complaint* didn't endure all these years simply for salacious reasons: the memorable, and now fading, generational scandal of his having depicted masturbation so graphically and with such confessional energy:

> So galvanic [explains Portnoy] is the effect of cotton
> panties against my mouth—so galvanic is the *word*
> "panties"—that the trajectory of my ejaculation
> reaches startling new heights: leaving my joint like
> a rocket it makes right for the light bulb overhead,
> where to my wonderment and horror, it hits and it
> hangs. Wildly in the first moment I cover my head,
> expecting an explosion of glass, a burst of flames—

disaster, you see, is never far from my mind. Then
quietly as I can I climb the radiator and remove the
sizzling gob with a wad of toilet paper. I begin a
scrupulous search of the shower curtain, the tub, the
tile floor, the four toothbrushes—God forbid!—and
just as I am about to unlock the door, imagining I
have covered my tracks, my heart lurches at the sight
of what is hanging like snot to the toe of my shoe. I
am the Raskolnikov of jerking off . . .

We ate this stuff up, for reasons we could hardly explain and didn't much want to. We were grateful to the
author of *Portnoy's Complaint* for what we took to be his
candor. But—though this may not have been obvious to
us at the time—we did not read such passages the way we
read the folded-over pages of Harold Robbins's *The Car-
petbaggers*. For Portnoy is not only a more sophisticated
raconteur than Robbins, he is never quite in league with
our fantasies, or his own, for that matter. In almost every
case, Eros always flies away and he is left with panic, then
cover-up, then ironic distance from crime and punishment, then despair over his sense of alienation ("in my
blindness and ecstasy, I got it all in the pompadour, like a
blast of Wildroot Cream Oil"; "I once cored an apple . . .
and ran off into the woods to fall upon the orifice of the
fruit, pretending that the cool and mealy hole was actually

between the legs of that mythical being who always called me Big Boy when she pleaded for what no girl in all recorded history had ever had"). The voice is self-consciously ironic, learned, avid.

"The book, clearly, was transgressive and utterly in its moment," the critic Igor Webb told me. "Who thought that you could write about masturbating in the bathroom while your mother was on the other side of the door—who thought you could write about this, and do so with that timbre, with its layers: the humor, the psychoanalytic frame, the elation. That was liberating but also curious. It was a thrill: humanizing of the taboo." Lacayo writes that for the masturbation alone *Portnoy's Complaint* "will endure forever," though he added, hinting at something, that this was because the scenes transcended their own calculated vulgarity to raise other, more permanent questions—say, painful tensions between children and parents ("Doctor, what should I rid myself of, tell me, the hatred . . . or the love?"). Portnoy, a literary agent friend wrote me, paved the way for the smartened-up, masturbation-rich film comedies by visible, young, almost always Jewish tricksters like Judd Apatow: "Those reluctant, barely grown-up guys would have nothing without Portnoy's now distant permission. And this is just one major commercial, cultural, long-distance service provided by the book. Convention-bound, expensive, big-ticket romantic comedies were allowed to be about the fussy, demented, frightened partings from the reassuring cleanliness of childhood."

Alfred Kazin had tried to summarize things early on when he reviewed *Portnoy's Complaint* in the *New York Review of Books* in the spring of 1969: "No matter where he goes and how many girls he can have at one time in his bed, [Portnoy] is still a masturbator at heart, still rebelling against the undefeatable."[5]

Masturbation as a form of rebellion, lewdness as a cultural opportunity, repression as a psychic fact. The complaint, in this surface sense, was hardly Portnoy's alone. The novel did not kick off the sixties, we thought, so much as provide a comic culmination for them. "There is no firm *language* for the adult male embarked on a career of voluptuous enjoyment," Kazin writes in his diaries, reading the galleys of *Portnoy's Complaint*. "He lies to no woman more than he lies to himself—lies in the sense that he improvises positions and postures (morally speaking) for him to live by in this hand-to-mouth existence."[6] Elia Kazan's film *Splendor in the Grass*, from 1961, had given us the tragic prelude, what was *then* the matter with Kansas: Bud and Deanie—Warren Beatty and Natalie Wood—hot for each other, gritting their teeth, going insane. By 1969, their shame was just on the verge of becoming quaint. Woodstock Nation had not yet sacked out, but Hef had had his Bunnies, Mrs. Robinson, her Ben, Jacqueline Susann's valley, its dolls. The literary scholar Robert Alter told me he recalls how by the early 1960s three novels—the reissue of *Lady Chatterley's Lover, Lolita,* and *Tropic of Cancer*—had pretty much broken "the last taboos against dealing with the erotic." Our carnality had been ratified in the many art-house cinemas where *Blow-up* and *Barbarella* had played. As for the B movies, the curve of Angie Dickinson's breasts was becoming as agreeably unavoidable as the Coca-Cola trademark.

Nor, after reading Saul Bellow's *Herzog,* could we, or at least the more studious among us, doubt Jewish complaining as an art form or an author's vehicle for condescending to the world. Many of us found ourselves rooting instinctively for Portnoy's impudence, for his comically Jewish version of Bud, for "letting it all hang out"—for expressing the dirt of desire after the hygiene of childhood—because we assumed nothing in the private sphere could be more shocking than what had been going on in the public. *Portnoy's Complaint* was polished up during the spring of 1968. This was the time of the Tet Offensive, Walter Cronkite's doubts, John and Yoko's liturgy, the gunning down of Dr. King, the tugs at RFK's cuffs, Soviet tanks in Prague, PLO hijackings, Cohn-Bendit, HAL, Chicago "police riots." The book was published during the months of numbness we felt when we realized how all of the above had yielded (I still wince to say it) President Richard M. Nixon. For educated Americans, not even particularly hip ones, there was suddenly internal exile to contemplate.

Todd Gitlin wrote in his great chronicle, *The Sixties*, that people who had been veterans of anti-war protest and political experiment "gravitated toward the milieu which in the late Sixties had begun to call itself the 'human potential movement.'"

> This melange of encounter groups, therapies, and mystical disciplines promised to uncover authentic selves, to help people "live in the present," "go with the flow," "give themselves permission," "free themselves of shoulds," "get in touch with their feelings," "get in touch with their bodies"—promises of relief for besieged individuals burdened by obligations; promises of intimate personal relations for those who had lost the hope of God or full community; promises of self-expression for the inhibited and cramped, the bored and spoiled.[7]

Turning inward, to a kind of sexual defiance, seemed political all by itself, maybe the only politics left to us. America had been softened up by Mike Nichols, by Mort Sahl—also by the wackiness that had trickled into America from England's *Beyond the Fringe* and Monty Python.

Our gang. In this atmosphere, what could be more welcome than an author doing to prudery what Sinclair Lewis had done to "modern merchandizing." Roth, so he told *Esquire*'s Scott Raab, had "let it rip."

I had written three books prior that were all careful in a way. Each was different from the other, but they didn't let it rip, and now was my chance. [*Portnoy's Complaint*] was written at the tail end of the sixties, so all that was happening around one, and I was living in New York at the time, so the theatrics around me gave me confidence. . . . I had a friend who had a strong influence on me, not as a writer, just as a friend. I was very fond of him; he was a terrific live wire—Al Goldman. He taught at Columbia. He wrote a classical-music column. He was very much a serious literature professor. . . . The sixties transformed him. I don't know anyone more transformed—and many people were transformed. Al became a rock-music critic for *Life*, and he was my rock instructor. He used to take me to Madison Square Garden when he was covering various people. . . . B. B. King came to the Garden, and Al took me backstage to meet him just after *Portnoy's Complaint* came out. The girls were lined up around the block for B. B. King's dressing room, and in back with him he had a half a dozen or

so acolytes in powder-blue suits, and we sat around
and talked for a while. Then I went to get the seat
while Al interviewed him further—and when I left,
B. B. King looked at his boys in their powder-blue
suits, rubbed my seat, and said, "This guy just made
a million dollars from *writin' a book*." . . . I went to
a Janis Joplin concert with him, I went to a Doors
concert with him—it was wonderful . . .[8]

So it seemed natural to think Portnoy's peculiar aban-
don was a turn of the screw from the author of *Goodbye,
Columbus*, his inhibitions removed by the vehemence of
anti-war radicalism. And, indeed, no stand-up comic before *Portnoy's Complaint* had got in there and talked this
way about that special discontent that unravels the civi-
lized: the fuse of pussy, the eruptions, the madness. We
couldn't let go of this Roth, our Prince of Pussy, whose
ability to endure freedom seemed a kind of standard, no
matter the toll it allegedly took on his sanity. We wanted
him, like Portnoy, to be in one affair after another, even
if this meant one shrink after another. We ignored Roth's
caution that he was inventing a character whose self-pity
and obscenity were *also* revealing.

The caution—that Portnoy was not Roth—was ignored even by more seasoned critics who read novels for
a living. "I want the novelist," wrote *New York Times* critic

Christopher Lehmann-Haupt, heaping praise on Roth for finding a way to say *everything he really feels* through his apparent alter ego, "to bare his soul, to stop playing games, to cease sublimating." And this being America, the book's lines, especially about masturbation, were probably most scandalous for people who never actually bothered to read them. Jacqueline Susann, who appeared on Johnny Carson in 1969, was asked if she had ever met Roth; after replying that she had not, she added that she would like to meet him but would "not want to shake his hand." (Years later, Roth was still consoling himself: "After all, it wasn't as if André Malraux said it to François Mauriac.")[9]

It did not easily occur to us, in short, that a book that was in its moment was not just of its moment; that one didn't really need the sixties to have the shame, or the family, or the confession, or the dangers of erotic insurgency; that unlike Sergeant Pepper, say, the book was not valorizing the sixties, but seemed preoccupied with resisting the misapplied moral lessons of the forties, or the pipe-and-elbow-patches intellectual styles of the fifties— resistance that *launched* the sixties. We found it hard to see that the book's themes were latent in any bourgeois decade, a point I'll return to in the next chapter. We also found it hard to see that, to have Portnoy, you needed Roth to be not just unbuttoned but inventive.

Roth would soon bore of being famous for "baring his soul." In New York, people threw him knowing looks as he passed them on the street. Jewish leaders were inflamed. Strangers at the swimming pool assumed that he, like Portnoy, was on the verge of seducing a lover or breaking up with one, offering him advice; diners at a restaurant would pass his table and ask if he was having liver. It was not like being famous for the Salk vaccine. "It was a story about a boy and his conscience," Herman Roth, Roth's (by then) widowed father, put the matter with a lovely simplicity to *People* magazine in 1983. "They blew it all out of proportion."[10]

Between 1971 and 1976, Roth often traveled to Prague, funneling money and book contracts to Czech writers, eventually founding a series for Penguin Books called "Writers from the Other Europe," which helped to get novels by Milan Kundera, Bruno Schultz, Tadeusz Borowski, and others into print. In Prague, the prestige of having written an international best-seller could be put to use; the further he got from New York, and the closer to ground zero of Jewish tragedy, the easier it was to escape being honored as America's preeminent Jewish sex-clown. Eventually, however, Roth felt he had to weigh in as a critic, raising questions about the perils of writing fiction, and especially *this* fiction. In the fall of 1974, he published a lengthy, earnest essay, "Imagining Jews," in the *New York Review of Books*. It focused largely on how contemporary Jewish writers had overcautiously rendered the impacted aggressions of sexuality, another subject worth returning to. But it began with Roth's confession of frustration with critics underestimating Portnoy as an invention.

Roth noted that critics praised the author of *Portnoy's Complaint* for sheer spontaneity one year, and, a year or two later (when "the pendulum of received opinion swung the other way"), praised "disguise, artifice, fantasy, montage, and complicated irony"—all the things *Portnoy's Complaint* was presumably lacking. He was adamant: fiction is never just one thing or another; the line between a confession and fiction is not easily drawn under any circumstance. ("When there is a writer in a family," Czeslaw Milosz says, "that family is finished.") Yet craft matters, intention matters—whatever the difficulties in divining it. Was it not time to think about what the character revealed and therefore what the author—not his character—was up to?

> For a writer like Grace Paley (or Mark Twain or Henry Miller), as for an actor like Marlon Brando, creating the illusion of intimacy and spontaneity is not just a matter of letting your hair down and being yourself, but of inventing a whole new idea of what

"being yourself" sounds like and looks like; "natural-ness" happens not to grow on trees. . . .

In the case of my own "confession," it did not diminish the voyeuristic kick—to call it by its rightful name—to remember that the novelist who was assumed to be baring his soul and ceasing to sublimate had formerly drawn a rather long, serious, even solemn face. Nor did it hurt that the subject which this supposed confession focused on at some length was known to one and all and publicly disowned by just about as many: masturbation. That this shameful, solitary addiction was described in graphic detail, and with gusto, must have gone a long way to attracting to the book an audience that previously had shown little interest in my writing.[11]

Roth might have added that, when it comes to the body, readers appreciative of literary invention have always had to push past peepers. American readers after World War I seemed to notice mostly Joyce's vocalization of Molly Bloom's sexual surrender, or Leopold Bloom's taking us to the toilet (pleased, the narrator tells us, that he is not left with the mild constipation he had felt the day before). American courts had kept *Ulysses* off book-sellers' shelves until 1933, as Australia had at first banned the sale of *Portnoy's Complaint*. Or think of the other putatively salacious books Alter mentioned—*Tropic of Cancer,* *Lolita*—all of which had run afoul of censors.

The judge who eventually ruled that *Ulysses* was *not* obscene had to give the term "stream of consciousness" a legal standing just to clear the path to its publication. He understood, sensibly, that Joyce's exposure of Bloom's particular intimacies had to be seen in the context of the effort to achieve a kind of genial intimacy. By 1966 the Supreme Court, led by Justice William Brennan, ruled that obscenity standards were virtually unenforceable, if they had ever been wise to begin with. Was it really too much to hope, Roth implied, that by 1969 educated Americans would have understood that the reports of emotion built around the masturbation in *Portnoy's Complaint* were not meant to be salacious except in the sense that, for a teenager, salacious was just what you'd expect and what teens grasp their actions in terms of? Then again, the sustained comic monologue made the novel a hit—not a problem that Joyce lived to have—which made it harder to take Roth seriously. *Portnoy's Complaint* touched more American nerves than any previous book about sex and in a more immediate way. What if not sales was proof of pulpable fiction? Random House had sold perhaps 35,000 copies of *Ulysses* by the end of 1934.[12]

This is not to suggest—Roth would not—that Joyce's magnified realism compares unfavorably to Portnoy's psychoanalytic burlesque. It *is* to suggest that Joyce's rendering of, say, Leopold Bloom's mind—the sound of a trolley leading to the memory of a corpse, to a passage from a remembered Bible class—is harder to stay with than Portnoy's stories. Bloom is thinking; Joyce's astonishing achievement was to make the associations seem convincingly serial, if not random. Roth, in contrast, is not rendering Portnoy's mind. He is rendering Portnoy's talk to a definite kind of listener. Both novels suggest enmeshment, but Portnoy's words are shaped into stories and arguments that others—the analyst and, by implication, readers familiar with psychoanalytic frames—are supposed to find convincing. The achievement is in making us believe the analyst would be awake to this special kind of confession; that Portnoy would understand his challenge was to *keep* his analyst awake. The naturalness of Portnoy's talk happens *not* to grow on trees.

This brings us around to the novel's great innovation. Can a few pitiably urgent and curiously deadpan scenes about masturbation—its collateral fantasies, its residual guilt—really be enough to send a book to the librarians' list of the century's hundred top novels, right there between *The Wind in the Willows* and *The Plague*? Yes, hell yes, but that's because they are nested in peculiarly unhinged revelations from the couch. *Psychoanalysis provided the vessel for everything. It takes the liberties for you.* Portnoy's job is to say everything that comes into his mind: he is melancholy and searching for a liberating forbearance. The presumption of his therapy is that he and his analyst are reflecting on human nature where he is the subject at hand; he cannot do justice to the encounter if he holds back. The moral condemnation comes neurotically, that is, comes first from Portnoy himself. Nothing is sacred because everything is material; the material implies "failure"; the comedy begins, if at all, here. In this one sense, *Portnoy's Complaint* clearly *was* a product of its time. By one estimate, there were over forty-five hundred practicing analysts in the United States by 1978.[13] Were there that many more qualified economists?

Perhaps the closest thing to *Portnoy's Complaint* in world literature to that time was *Confessions of Zeno* by Italo Svevo, published in 1923. This novel is written in the form of a diary (admittedly "full of lies") kept by the protagonist for his analyst. The diary admits to obsessive relations with women (and cigarettes) and is published by the analyst, vengefully, after Zeno terminates his visits. *Confessions of Zeno* was championed by Joyce but never achieved much success. It was simply ahead of its time: the audience wasn't big enough to get the point. And *Portnoy's Complaint* then shaped its time. America was not the same place after Portnoy's talk had fully sunk in. It was a place of carnal knowledge. It taught young people "to think." Consider how Garrison Keillor's own little chronicles of Lutheran dinner tables have come to seem so edgy. There would be no barb unless audiences had come to understand that macaroni casseroles represented "repression." You have to presuppose a great many people supplying the tragedy while the protagonist supplies the comedy.

By the way, it seems no accident (as Dr. Spielvogel might say) that both patients and stand-up comics will use the word "material" in this context. The writer Adam Gopnik told me that *Portnoy's Complaint* drives home how thin the line is between the psychoanalytic session and improvised comedy: both have confessional vigor, strategic self-deprecation, angry revelations about (if not denunciation of) intimates, juxtapositions of previously unassociated frames of reference. A classic stand-up routine often seems calculated to seem mad. The voice is meant to sound so perceptive and unbuttoned that it can't be bothered to listen to what it is saying. (*They laughed when I said I would be a comedian. Well, they're not laughing now!*)

And, as it happens, *Portnoy's Complaint* grew out of a kind of stand-up routine. In the early 1960s, Roth had come to the Upper East Side after teaching a stint at the Iowa Writers' Workshop, mainly to recover from the stresses of his famously turbulent marriage to—and divorce from—Margaret Martinson. By 1963, he was well started in analysis with a well-known psychiatrist who had many writers and artists for patients, Dr. Hans Kleinschmidt. Roth was also good company to a group of male friends, including not only Goldman but also Robert Brustein, the theater director, and Jason Epstein, his editor at Random House. In time, having marinated in the language of psychoanalysis, and soaked in some of the sixties, Roth began to perform sketches and do shtick, imagining what an analysis of a particular, mythological Jewish man would *really* sound like. "These grew, a little manically, sometimes lasting fifteen minutes, sometimes going on all night." Roth would perform at the Brusteins' dinner table, or at Jason and Barbara Epstein's. He finally started asking himself if it might be possible to write like this.

The gestation period for the novel, David Remnick writes (in a profile published in the *New Yorker* in 2000), was "long, complicated and chaotic." Its first incarnation was a two-hundred-page riff called "Jewboy," based on a Newark childhood. Then came the draft of a play called "The Nice Jewish Boy," which was read as a workshop exercise at the American Place Theater in 1964, with an as-yet undiscovered Dustin Hoffman in the main role. After completing *When She Was Good* in 1966, Roth wrote a monologue "beside which"—he told Remnick—"the fetid indiscretions of *Portnoy's Complaint* would appear to be the work of Louisa May Alcott." Then came yet another manuscript, "Portrait of an Artist," in which the family Portnoy makes its first appearance. Finally—the breakthrough—a story titled "The Jewish Patient Begins His Analysis," whose setting was the psychiatrist's office. This gave the rage and obscenity, what Remnick calls the "performance-piece comedy," a literary frame.[14]

The novel was not, in other words, a simple recasting of a spontaneous performance. Roth (as he told Plimpton in that launch interview) was influenced not by stand-up comics like Lenny Bruce so much as by "sit-down comics like Franz Kafka." The stage is a place where the comedian engages directly with the audience, goes after famous people, or recognizable manners, or ideologies, or affects a pathetic way of being (you see Don Rickles, or Robin Williams, or Sarah Silverman, and you know where you are supposed to stand with respect to *them*). The couch, however contrived, is a place for details about a particular life, a particular web of relations, that discourages judgment of this kind. You expect to learn from hearing what's going on, but not form opinions about the patient. Of course you *do* form opinions, but these may change over the years. The grid of relations called a "life" is a shifting, forgivable abstraction. "I needed permission," Roth told Remnick, as he had told the Bard students, "and permis-

sion came with casting the book as a psychoanalytic confession." The rule here is that there are no rules: "the rule
here is no restraint, the rule here is no decorum."

Roth did not intend to reproduce something like a real
analytic session. This is a very stylized abstraction. (Any
former patient would know that Portnoy's sessions are
too productive to be realistic.) Yet the couch gave Roth
permission to concentrate on the details of Portnoy's
physicality, to show a man spinning his wheels, incapable
of getting to where he wants to go, precisely because
of the *shmutzig* facts of his body and the creatures from
his past embedded within. Even more pitiable, Portnoy
thinks he is *supposed* to disentangle himself. He has not yet
learned that he can only age out of his condition. Roth is
implying, slyly, that Portnoy is still callow, and one feature of his being haunted is his determination not to be.
You age out of that, too.

Unlike a great comedian, then, Portnoy projects a per-
sona that may grow on you but not with you. When I first
read the novel, I, too, could barely understand why Roth
would want to dissociate himself from Portnoy's grievances, so brilliant, brave, and entertaining did I find every
one. When I read the novel again in my thirties, I *feared* I
was Portnoy and my children would become the victims
of my "neurotic" perceptions. More recently, reading it
once again for this book, what struck me was how sad and

young Portnoy sounded. I still believed every word of his slanted talk. But what seemed daring when I was twenty seemed merely touching when I was sixty. I vaguely wanted to reassure him, or smack him, or both.

A word about the virtuosity with which the psychoanalytic talk is affected. Stylized as the narrator is, any analysand would immediately sense the way his associations constitute a kind of imaginative network, each woven crossing entailing the other, something you might well reproduce if you were lying there yourself. "The realism is of a peculiar kind," Roth's teaching notes continue. "It is limited: expressionistic realism of a very coarse variety combined with the grotesque conception of life that is the family satire . . . the ugly aggression of satire." You can't complain that it is too awful, he says. Given the psychoanalytic frame, criticism would be justified if it weren't awful enough. Decorum will only bottle things up.

You start with the grievance, then move to the fantasy of retribution, then to guilt, and then to an original childhood fear. You dwell on the fear and then, in a tribute to the safety of the couch, move to sadness. As you search for the sources of sadness, you uncover memory, which provokes feelings of poignancy, of loving connection, then hunger, then erotic charges, then loss, and then new—or putatively new—grievance. The stories and observations fall back on themselves: you get stuck on a word—"brassiere," say—and the moment you speak it, the word tangles in your head with other words. You start with pain, burrow into dirt, get to memory, and end with motive.

Take the chapter Roth calls "Whacking Off," where most of the funniest passages about masturbation are served up. Portnoy begins by telling us the ways in which he found himself "wholly incapable of keeping my paws from my dong," while a mythical being pleads for Big Boy. This leads to the famous butcher shop, and then to a discovery of a little dot on his penis, which was *certainly* cancer—the only fit punishment for the crime of violating his family's dinner. Now that he's introduced the idea that he is his own Raskolnikov, a mature, ironic erudition intrudes. My God, what is freedom and what merely shaking the bars? Suddenly, with Spielvogel attending, Portnoy's consciousness is invaded by the primal Mommy—her magical tits and powers of comfort never stripped out of experience—knocking at the bathroom door, asking to inspect stools that may betray unkosher *fressing.* Big Boy turns into a putative child, and therefore a deeply underestimated male, as humiliated and tragic as any rapist. Which leads reimagined little Portnoy to defiance and then to guilty thoughts of disloyalty to his father, as his mother finally reduces him to tears. ("Success. I am crying. There is no good reason for me to be crying, but in this household everybody tries to get a good cry in at least once a day.")

The drama does not end there. Thoughts of the father lead to thoughts of supersession, culminating in memories of emancipation at college, of Wordsworth and ambition. But this leads to new guilty rushes—can I go to college and leave my parents behind?—and then nearly metaphysical thoughts of being so hedged in by Jewish law, so in pursuit of "the mean," that Maimonides would be positively *kvelling*. The laws of kashrut are yanked from the world of celebration of the divine and plunked into the world of adolescent taboo:

> Look, am I exaggerating to think it's practically miraculous that I'm ambulatory? The hysteria and the superstition! The watch-its and the be-carefuls! You mustn't do this, you can't do that—hold it! don't! you're breaking an important law! *What* law? *Whose* law? They might as well have had plates in their lips and rings through their noses and painted themselves blue for all the human sense they made! Oh, and the *milchiks* and *flaishiks* besides, all those *meshuggeneh* rules and regulations on top of their own private craziness! It's a family joke that when I was a tiny

child I turned from the window out of which I was watching a snowstorm, and hopefully asked, "Momma, do we believe in winter?"

Raging?—yes. Funny?—in context, very. Maddeningly random?—not exactly. For there is nothing really free about the associations here. One thing leads to another because, at least in psychoanalytic terms, each thought *follows* from the other. In *Ulysses*, you can snatch passages from Bloom's reasoning at almost any point and get a sense of the man—not the whole man, perhaps, but the qualities from which the whole might be extrapolated. Yet quoting even paragraphs from *Portnoy's Complaint* inevitably means taking passages out of context and missing the point somewhat. Portnoy's monologues go on for pages and build like a Bruckner symphony. They have phases, movements, links. The patient presents a particular type of thinking. The reader comes to *expect* a particular type of thinking.

The book assumes the primal evolution that moves us from Eros to Autonomy; complaint is funny here because it's so determined by what "growth" means to Freudians ("Stop saying 'poopie' to me—I'm in high school!"). Readers, too, assume a ladder of development in the background, so that the foreground takes on a peculiar poignancy: the milk-fed calf touches our heart because we know he is trying to become a bull. Oh, and the book remains comic only because we know all along that our hero has had something of a provisionally acceptable ending, that he *survived*. Why, he has even become a human rights lawyer working for the mayor of New York—the Commissioner of Human Opportunity! (The Monkey, raging at him, calls him nothing but "Commissioner of Cunt"!) The point is, for all his presumed misery, and insistence on having been warped, he is not a serial murderer about to get the chair.

Again, the enigmatic strength of the writing was bound to cause Roth a certain misery. Critics and readers— especially those with only a glancing familiarity with his work—were bound to assume that nothing this confessional-*sounding* could be contrived. Presumably, if the voice was the voice of Portnoy, the hand was the hand of Roth. It was all too easy—because Roth made things *look* easy—to assume that Roth's mother was the model for Sophie, his father for Portnoy's father, his sister for his sister, and so on. It was easy to believe the rumor, which dogged Roth for months, that the author of *Portnoy's Complaint* had had a crack-up. The thing is, Roth did not *have* a sister. Nor was he particularly despondent after writing a runaway best-seller, though his notoriety was not quite as gracious as the one he had hoped for. As for crack-ups, these come and go, and every sane writer has had his or her share. But you would know that from *reading* Roth, would you not? An abundance of self-consciousness will do that to you.

Perhaps the most curious thing about the confusion of Roth with his protagonist was that the young author had signaled his skeptical fascination with Portnoy-like grieving eight years before. Any critic who had bothered to read Roth's own criticism would have known this. Though he had not yet committed to any psychoanalytic framing, in 1961 Roth had identified the template that engendered Portnoy's "perversion" (passive father, voluble mother, little *shmendrick* screaming in the middle), and wondered just how this had become a kind of folklore. It had jumped out at him in the stories of many of his students, especially male Jewish students at the Iowa Writers' Workshop, in the late fifties and early sixties. "The Jewish boy," Roth had written in an article called "Some New Jewish Stereotypes," published in 1961 in *American Judaism*,

> is watched at bedtime, at study time, and especially at meal time. Who he is watched by is his mother. The father we rarely see, and between him and the boy there seems to be little more than a nodding acquaintance. The old man is either working or sleeping or across the table, silently stowing it away. Still there is a great deal of warmth in these families—especially

when compared to the Gentile friend's family—and almost all of it is generated by the mother. And it does not strike the young hero the way it strikes Harry Golden and his audience. The fire that warms can also burn and asphyxiate: what the hero envies the Gentile boy is his parents' *indifference*, and largely, it would seem, because of the opportunities it affords him for sexual adventure. Religion here is understood, not as the key to the mysteries of the divine and the beyond, but to the mystery of the sensual and the erotic, the wonder of laying a hand on the girl down the street.[15]

Again, the worst thing about confusing Roth with Portnoy was missing how constructed the novel was. One did not write such fiction without gathering string for it over a good number of years. And the confusion began in underestimating, not the stringency of Roth's sexual decorum (which was as negotiable as any reader's), but his literary discipline. *Portnoy's Complaint* was trying to achieve something, or at least was meant to unsettle something. There is truth bouncing off the walls of the analytical room, but it is one person's shaped-and-bent truth— really many inconsistent truths—collected by passions the way filings are collected by a magnet. The setting suggests detailed, gripping, funny judgments. At the same time, the room suggests *no point of view from which to evaluate whether the judgments are remotely accurate or fair.* To judge—or judge prematurely—would not be in the culture of psychoanalysis. No other literary premise gives us what is so coarse about people yet leaves us so unable to distance ourselves from them. The patient's vain idea that he can escape his many snares is a big part of what's comical.

The classics of confessional literature led you somewhere considerably more redemptive. Augustine shares his perverse thoughts, especially as a young man, but we are invited to believe that these thoughts are, precisely, perverse: a passing, sinful stage before conversion. Rousseau's *Confessions* suggest a path to revelation of a different kind: liberated sensuousness, primal action. And one has very much the same feeling of being led—only stronger, given the sad twists of Flaubert's plot—listening to Emma Bovary's thoughts through the narrator's voice. You feel, given your own carnality, that Emma's fate could indeed be yours. But you also feel, given your *knowledge* of Emma's fate, that your carnality can yield a very different fate. Her tragedy is there to save your life, make it more of a comedy, or so you think. (Old joke: An ancient comes out of a performance of *Oedipus Rex*, sobbing and sobbing; his companion comes over and says, "I'm so glad you enjoyed it!")

Even in *Ulysses*, much of what we are confronted with—the whole load of uncensored thought attributed to Stephen, Leopold, and Molly—is mostly reported to us by a subtle narrator, penetrating the interstices of action and mind. This leaves us both edified and perplexed, wondering what to make of the consciousness of the narrator. But the reader, along with the hovering voice, has been given a kind of out. We listen to the characters thinking and speaking and find many points of identification, even empathy; but if things become too disturbing for us we can simply retreat to the idea that we, like the narrator, might be more knowing or just better off than the dramatis personae. After all, if the narrator can know so many things about other people, does this not mean that we readers can improve ourselves just overhearing others? Can we not, like writers, perfect our fate, think the thoughts of others *who cannot think ours?*

There is an amusing moment in Stephen Sondheim's musical play *Into the Woods*, when the characters, facing their various forms of impending doom, become conscious of the narrator off to the side of the stage, telling their story to the theater audience with a tsk-tsk in his voice. Suddenly they turn on him and offer him up to *his* doom. You laugh nervously, but thereafter the play becomes wonderfully unhinged: what promised to be a morality tale suddenly is a stage full of people who are no more than working hypotheses: voices clashing with one another, characters getting in and out of fixes or dying in the attempt; characters left with nothing but the comforts of the affection they give one another. Something like that feeling accompanies you almost from the first page of *Portnoy's Complaint* and stays with you until the very last line.

Let us review the bidding. *Portnoy's Complaint* piggybacked on the rowdiness of the sixties. Its psychoanalytic play caught the fancy of a generation familiar at last with Freudian ideas. The masturbation passages got readers' attention all right, but what eventually became clearer was that they were built into a fictional architecture that allowed them to seem, not the making of an individual's shame, but the marker of a bourgeois contradiction— about which more presently. Few of us looked for any such high intention, at least at first, since the writing seemed so natural one imagined the author was simply emptying his mind, much as his protagonist had. But the more we began to see the novel as—how did Roth's father put it?—the exploration of a "boy and his conscience," the more enigmatic the book became.

What conventions were undermined by Portnoy's inescapable desire, mostly braided with (barely repressed) aggression, and arguably leading to self-destruction? Had happiness become a big joke? How, if at all, did Portnoy's

Jewish origins reinforce *that* question? Did Portnoy's psychoanalytic knowledge really provide him any kind of answer? Each step in the interrogation exposed a new object of complaint. Portnoy moves from mocking the bourgeois family, to Jews, to psychoanalysis, while he remains himself an object of his mockery. Like Russian dolls, each object of satire is brightly painted and nested inside the one before. Let's start with the first.

CHAPTER TWO

Really Icky

Portnoy as Satirist

Alfred Kazin, remember, paid our hero an oblique tribute in his 1969 review, calling Portnoy a "masturbator at
heart," whom he rushed to dignify as a man in rebellion
against "the undefeatable."

> Portnoy in heat is particularly funny. Even when he
> graduates from the nearest receptacle to other bodies,
> sex remains his favorite form of protest. In the wildest
> throes, his bitterness is more in evidence than his
> passion, and his life remains, as always, furiously
> mental. . . . All this reaches its right voice and pitch
> and end (though there is no end) in the comic situa-
> tion of Portnoy who at thirty-three, no matter where
> he goes and how many girls he can have at one time

in his bed, is still a masturbator at heart, still rebelling against the undefeatable, still seething against
MaMa . . .[1]

What "rebellion" and what's so "mental" about it?
These seemed threads worth pulling. Kazin observed earlier in the review that "in a country so crammed and lively
with jostling human styles, languages, traditions, races, it
is most practical as well as sophisticated to recognize one's
role, to see on every hand how different a role can be." Yet
Kazin begged his own good question, leaving Portnoy's
"role" to the imaginations of *New York Review* readers, a
great many of whom were liberal Jews; he was content, it
seemed, to focus empathy on young Jews who thought
themselves "born not to faith but to a neurosis, a 'condition,' a burden . . ." For our part, the readers, we intui-
tively understood Kazin, or so we thought, or were em-
barrassed to admit that we did not, and so remained.

Anyway, I want to pursue the point Kazin left aside:
call it "the politics of masturbation," though just writing
the phrase feels as dangerously earnest as an SDS meet-
ing back in 1969. And I pursue it because Portnoy's "role"
could never be understood by intuition alone. In the previous chapter, I argued that the novel's outer layer of satire became most immediately sensational, for the object
of mockery seemed, vaguely, how the Jewish family be-

came a theater of "repression" for a young man's ordinary sexual ardor. Portnoy appeared the satirist and Roth was rashly assumed to be his sly agent. Yet "seething against MaMa" always implied a more general target—anyway, never a merely parochial one, not even from the start. Yes, Portnoy's "style" was Jewish, but that was not all there was to his role. Roth had his eye on America.

Acolytes of psychoanalysis might have supposed that Kazin's implied question ("rebellion against what?") was more or less superfluous, since every new cohort, everywhere, passed through the developmental torments of childhood, and dirty minds would have formed spontaneously in each adorable little Oedipus. Rebellion was against growing up. Yet when Kazin also wrote of Portnoy being "furiously mental," he was acknowledging a protagonist who *was* grown up, somebody with a head on his shoulders: a tormenting social consciousness with political responsibilities, not just sexual fantasies. For Kazin, Portnoy was no Harpo, whistling and groping himself back into the oceanic feeling. Portnoy's "protest" pertained to his life as a man. Actually Kazin writes contemporaneously in his journal what he might have liked to publish in his review:

Roth and A.K. Eat, eat my child, eat! So one recovers in bed, either with another or oneself, . . . with the

penis used as a fork or spoon to shovel the gratification. Somewhere in earliest childhood one sucked and
was sucked; all parts of that primal female body were
available to us. . . . [I]n a time of unlimited consumer
satisfaction in so many things, when people are indeed
hipped on getting, enjoying, moving, feeling with
the swirl, when the difference between the sexes are
always breaking down, when the one-body principle
seems to be acting as flatly as the one earth-space . . .
—how can one explain that the male is committed
to his *enjoyment,* to his freedom and movement—in
a word, to his infant nostalgia?[2]

Others sensed the political implications, too. The
writer James Carroll, a newly minted Paulist priest in the
late 1960s, told me he read *Portnoy's Complaint* as a revelation: "It felt like I was reading something forbidden. I
remember exactly where I was, the summer of 1969, at
the Paulist vacation spa at Lake George, New York. I sat
against a tree, with worn, gnarled roots—the same summer I read *Marjorie Morningstar,* actually, which I knew to
be a cartoon—anyway, here I was a celibate Catholic
male, for whom sex was forbidden, surrounded, I felt, by
sexual license in the imaginations of fervent young Jews.
Portnoy's Complaint was absolutely rooting to *me.* The *political* claim of it, the unabashed idea that sexuality was

central to human experience, when everything in my world was insisting it was marginal. Portnoy was the perfect foil of the world *I* was living in." Nelson Aldrich remembers: "As a sort of boarding school repressed WASP, where any kind of sexuality was icky, really icky—not bad necessarily; one had *evolved*—but sex was a big, serious point of vulnerability, a matter of social decency—anyway, for Roth to send that up with such ribaldry—oh God, what a blessing!"

A mixed blessing, obviously. Kazin adds in his journal, as if summarizing Dr. Spielvogel's diagnosis, that given how many "forces and traditions contend in him," a man's "longings for . . . pure gratification are intermixed with shocks and guilts and, above all, *uncertainties.*" Kazin was shrewd to steer us toward thoughts of "social decency," which, not surprisingly, is as debatable now in America as it ever was. Sure, irreverence was de rigueur at the end of the sixties, what with Nixon in the White House, universities exploding with ideological fervor, the establishment exposed as The Establishment, and so forth. But that was foreground. Kazin was suggesting that there was also a residual background, an American normal: a world in which George Bailey is kissing Zuzu's petals and Willy Loman is asking for a raise. What was this, generation after generation? What observance was suggested by Portnoy's breach?

■

I asked Roth about this, why *he* thought his book out-lasted the scandal over Portnoy's masturbation, or at least what larger social critique might be inferred from Port-noy's satiric fuming. He answered, cautiously: "*Épater le bourgeois*, bourgeois shock—people still have that from the book, though God knows what hasn't been said or written, or what kids haven't since been told is an 'ac-cepted part of life.'" (Then he added, in German-inflected falsetto: "*Darling, you ahrre not masturrbating enough!*")

Roth's answer surprised as well as amused me. Portnoy was no Baudelaire, not proud of his decadence—quite the opposite, alas—nor was his complaint about living in the middle class. More important, does it not seem a bit rushed to assume that "American" implies bourgeois, and bourgeois, prudish? Roth's own automatic riff on Dr. Ruth implied that, since the sixties, everyone from the surgeon general to Larry King has seemed willing to talk about teens masturbating as if going to a Pilates class. Why shock?

Yet Roth is surely right that the career of *Portnoy's Complaint* exposed yet again how ambivalent bourgeois America remains about sexuality, or about the social im-plications of strong sexual desire—a Yankee ambivalence about which *les bourgeois d'origine* persist in being amused. As I was writing this book, Eliot Spitzer hounded himself out of politics and Tiger Woods, still struggling to get his game back, put himself into sex therapy to face his "issues." (One can only imagine his eventual interview with Oprah, holding hands with some enchanting new love to whom he is "committed," perhaps talking about masturbation as a kind of gateway drug. And I haven't even started in on Republicans.)

There is a segment on *This American Life*, reported by the sardonic John Hodgman, in which young people were asked to imagine themselves superheroes, and were then asked which of two superpowers they would prefer, flying or invisibility. The respondents were about evenly split. The flyers, Hodgman slyly concludes, are people prepared to cut into the world: poised, intrepid, unashamed of sexual play. The invisibles are, in contrast, deeply curious but cautious, self-disciplined: observant, systematic, "secret masturbators." Anyway, it is the evenness of the split that seems most telling. The legendary sociologist Daniel Bell once called this split "the cultural contradiction of capitalism": an American normal that seems an oscillation between fear of flying and anger at invisibility.[3]

We were roaring in the twenties, depressed in the thirties, *noire* in the forties, uptight in the fifties, groovy in the sixties—we named American decades as if they expressed some cosmic morality play, where the pleasure principle bangs up against the reality principle, the latter often boiling down to a dip in the business cycle. Say the phrase "bourgeois American" and traditional images of renunciation spring to mind, the Age of Innocence with no clear end, the influence of residual Victorian habits, or Puritan notions of flesh and sin, evangelical fervor, the desire for stability, and so forth. But say "bourgeois freedom" and equally powerful images spring to mind: seduction, display, "making it." You don't need Paris in the springtime; just open *Sports Illustrated* in February. What happens in Vegas doesn't really stay in Vegas, does it?

There is a history to this ambivalence. A century before Nathaniel Hawthorne, Benjamin Franklin did not think it necessary to hide *his* "cunt craziness." He wrote the following to a young friend about the virtues of older women:

> The Face first grows lank and wrinkled; then the Neck; then the Breast and Arms; the lower Parts continuing to the last as plump as ever: So that covering all above with a Basket, and regarding only what is below the Girdle, it is impossible of two Women to know an old from a young one. And as in the dark all Cats are grey, the Pleasure of corporal Enjoyment with an old Woman is at least equal, and frequently superior, every Knack being by Practice capable of Improvement.

Okay, this was a private letter, not a novel, but a letter that had been famous for over two centuries, at times brought out to the sun, at times buried. Nobody imagined Franklin's sensibility could ever disappear; but extroversion about Enjoyment would come and go. Franklin was public enough about his awakened senses during his stay in France (where he met with, among others, Voltaire). At times, enlightenment meant tact, at times, the absence of shame. What happened in Versailles didn't exactly stay in Versailles. And from the beginning of the republic, the American middle class—"capable of Improvement"—tiptoed around sexual desire pretty much the way it tiptoed around naked ambition.

Here is the important point. Our shock is not from indecency, but from the absence of self-possession, the ultimate bourgeois possession. Our allergy is not to sexual desire but to the falling away of restraint. If Portnoy is our satirist, he is satirizing this. There are, as Franklin implied, things bourgeois men want all the time but feel more or less inhibited admitting to or pursuing in public. The dangers are latent; the first books that show *how* latent become indispensable. After reading Stephen Crane's *The Red Badge of Courage*, could Americans ever again discuss why we go to war without thinking of Henry Fleming's eagerness? After *Elmer Gantry*, who could speak of God without knowing the gullibility of religious congregations? Well, who after reading *Portnoy's Complaint* could speak the word "love" without thinking of Alex Portnoy's desire to plank a wilderness of Monkeys?

"I think it's safe to say I've dated a few Alexander Portnoys," the critic Alana Newhouse, wiser but sadder, told National Public Radio on the fortieth anniversary of the novel's publication. "I also know a few female Alexandra Portnoys . . ." *Portnoy's Complaint*, in this offhand sense, immediately became a point on the American compass, desire's magnetic north. What was undefeatable was the political contradiction of wanting reliability and wanting per se. The social contract required people to be motivated by selfish aggression, but also a sense of permanence, fidelity—"guilts." With Portnoy, we learned that predictability is where erections go to die. (Portnoy's college love Kay Campbell, after her "false alarm" missed period, became to him, he says, "boringly predictable in conversation, and about as desirable as blubber in bed.") David Lynch's sexual predator in his 1986 film *Blue Velvet* faces the film's callow young hero and tells him, "You're just like me!" Could we imagine just what the creep meant by this had the tracks laid down by *Portnoy's Complaint* not become grooved by then?

Perhaps our most vivid anticipation of what Portnoy took on came from D. H. Lawrence, in his remarkable attack on (of all people) Benjamin Franklin. This appeared in his freewheeling book *Studies in Classic American Literature*, published in 1923. Franklin may have been a libertine, but his overall sensibility was suffocating. The natural pleasures of selfishness must come up against engineered restraint. "Old Daddy Franklin," Lawrence shudders, was the first "downright American." He drew up for himself a creed that would keep our wolves in check. But it's the tameness that will kill us:

> Which of the various me's do you propose to educate, and which do you propose to suppress? . . . Oh, but I have a strange and fugitive self shut out and howling like a wolf or a coyote under the ideal windows. See his red eyes in the dark? This is the self who is coming into his own.

Franklin made himself a list of thirteen commandments which, Lawrence says, "he trotted inside like a grey nag in a paddock": "Why, the soul of man is a vast forest, and all Benjamin intended was a neat back garden." The last five on Franklin's list speak most powerfully to the subject at hand:

9. MODERATION
   Avoid extremes, forbear resenting injuries as much as you think they deserve.

10. CLEANLINESS

Tolerate no uncleanliness in body, clothes, or habitation.

11. TRANQUILLITY

Be not disturbed at trifles, or at accidents common or unavoidable.

12. CHASTITY

Rarely use venery but for health and offspring, never to dulness, weakness, or the injury of your own or another's peace or reputation.

13. HUMILITY

Imitate Jesus and Socrates.[4]

Lawrence admired Franklin well enough: his sturdiness, his sagacity, his "glimpsing into the thunders of electricity," his common sense and good humor—"All the qualities of a great man, and never more than a great citizen." Yet even today, you take a quick look at Franklin's commandments and you can almost feel Lawrence bridling. What can be more sickening than carnal health? What about prowling? "Middle-sized, sturdy, snuff-coloured Doctor Franklin, one of the soundest citizens that ever trod or 'used venery,'" Lawrence writes. He feared that savages would be extirpated "in order to make room for the cultivators of the earth." Franklin, even as a child, was nothing if not cultivated, his chickens never counted before they were hatched. For all his revolutionary politics, Franklin had cut the family life down to size (and, not coincidentally, lost the loyalty of a son in the process). His soundness was his sin against nature.

From the start of his career, Roth served notice that he, too, would target the trappings of bourgeois security—for example, his character "Mr. Russo," the ingenuous teacher in an early story, "You Can't Tell a Man by the Song He Sings," who believed (before it utterly compromised him) in "neatness, honesty, punctuality, planned destinies—who believed in the future, in Occupations!" Roth circled back to this theme in "Imagining Jews." Nobody, "not even a Jew," he writes, could mount a successful fight against "non-negotiable demands of crude antisocial appetite and vulgar aggressive fantasy." And Roth writes not *even* a Jew because by the time *Portnoy's Complaint* came along, American Jews had become something like the poster children for the kind of restraint and public decorum that the word "bourgeois" conveyed.

Jews had acquired an unprecedented moral prestige in the postwar American public. That's precisely what would help Roth make them a means to take on the American public. Jewish families in Europe had suffered from the unspeakable bloody-mindedness of others. They had worked hard and educated themselves, made the most of their rights. Emma Lazarus had given voice to the Statue of Liberty. Immigrant and first-generation Jews were prominently for the underdog, the unions, the fight against fascism. Liberal activism meant vigilance against anti-Semitism, yes, but also much more: "Our heroes were Roosevelt, La Guardia, and Brandeis," Roth says; "we were against the Republican oppressor."

In the fifties and early sixties, America had had a bead on the Jews, and a certain respectability was taken for granted. There was *The Goldbergs* from the radio, then television comedians who seemed the embodiment of playful patriotism: Phil Silvers, Milton Berle. There was Ed Sullivan, the host of hosts, introducing teasers like Sam Levinson and Myron Cohen. Later on Sunday night Jack Benny appeared, perhaps with George Burns—comics you weren't sure were Jewish, but who seemed the leaders of packs, and mock-sighed through contretemps with wives and sidekicks who clearly were not. Hollywood served up images of Jewish lawyers and doctors and agents who kept their heads while others didn't: Elizabeth Taylor and Sammy Davis Jr. went down into crisis and came up converted. The Jewish soda-fountain owner lamented the violence afflicting the Sharks and the Jets. The only rabbi everyone knew was Abraham Joshua Heschel, his white beard a gleaming contrast beside Martin Luther

King. The Weavers sang Israeli folksongs along with ballads from the Spanish Civil War.

But here was a book that seemed to say you don't have to be *this* respectful. I'm going to tell you about the repellent side, or at least about a man who is in a struggle with the repellent. ("The socially and morally repellent is his problem and lies at the root of his anguish.") The American embodiment of self-restraint cannot restrain himself, at least not in private, where lovers and analysts learn the truth. What's the lesson, then, for humanity? Portnoy, as satirist, implies that we should think about ourselves less condescendingly. "Can we let him speak," Roth's notes continue, "Can we listen?" Can we let Portnoy in, not into our lives, not into our living rooms, not into our families, but into literature? This kind of book had never been tried before in America, except by anti-Semites. But this was not ant-Semitism. It was a book. "The only throat down which I tried to shove this guy was the throat of literature. Some said, yes, why not?—some said, no, absolutely not."

Jews, Portnoy raged, controlled themselves so well— sure, partly because they had been a scorned minority and had learned to ingratiate themselves—but also because they had a religious culture that could seem an endless restraining order. One could so easily imagine Portnoy

approaching Franklin's list and, for all the Protestant re-
finements, detecting the scent of a confining *Halacha*.

> What else, I ask you, were all those prohibitive
> dietary rules and regulations all about to begin with,
> what else but to give us little Jewish children practice
> in being repressed? Practice, darling, practice, prac-
> tice, practice . . . Why else the two sets of dishes?
> Why else the kosher soap and salt? Why else, I ask
> you, but to remind us three times a day that life is
> boundaries and restrictions if it's anything, hundreds
> of thousands of little rules laid down by none other
> than None Other . . . And it doesn't make any differ-
> ence either (this I understand from the outset, about
> the way this God, Who runs things, reasons) how big
> or how small the rule is that you break: it's the break-
> ing alone that gets His goat—it's the simple fact of
> waywardness, and that alone, that He absolutely
> cannot stand, and which He does not forget either,
> when He sits angrily down (fuming probably, and
> surely with a smashing miserable headache, like my
> father at the height of his constipation) and begins
> to leave the names out of that book [of Life].

In another early story, Roth had served notice also that
he doubted the possibility of Jewish compliance being
sustained. "Is it me? Is it me ME ME ME ME!"—so his

little hero Ozzie, defying his rabbi, running naughtily to the roof of his school, worries, exhilarated, in "Conversion of the Jews." The narrator then adds: "It is the question a thief must ask himself the night he jimmies open his first window, and it is said to be the question with which bridegrooms quiz themselves before the altar." (Kazin's journal: "Glutton. Be committed to me alone, she says, love me for myself alone. But how can one explain to her that it is Woman one loves, the feminine principle as the necessity to gratification?")

Which brings me to Portnoy's greatest complaint, the one against the most chafing of middle-class institutions, the most foundational and easiest to lose. I am speaking, of course, of marriage.

If Roth's novel was shocking, this is because it played into perennial fears that, when bourgeois sexual restraint goes, so does the rearing family—not such an exaggerated fear as things turned out. The rate of divorce for males in 1900 was 84 per 100,000 and 114 per 100,000 for women. By 1950, the rate was at 1,070 per 100,000 for men and 1,373 per 100,000 for women; by 1980, rates for men had grown to 4,539 per 100,000 and 6,577 per 100,000 for women. The big jump had come in the 1970s, when no-fault divorce was first made legal.[5] *Portnoy's Complaint* would seem to have given no-fault its most comprehensive elaboration:

At least I don't have to get into bed every night with somebody who by and large I fuck out of obligation instead of lust. I mean, the nightmarish depression some people suffer at bedtime . . . I must admit that there is maybe, from a certain perspective, something a little depressing about my situation, too. . . . Only *why* should it end! To please a father and mother? . . . So what's the crime? Sexual freedom? In this day and age? Why should *I* bend to the bourgeoisie? . . . [A]ll the unconscious can do anyway, so Freud tells us, is *want. And* want! *And* WANT! Oh, Freud, do I know! . . . In the end, I just cannot take that step into marriage. But why should I? *Why?* . . . Imagine it: suppose I were to go ahead and marry A, with her sweet tits and so on, what will happen when B appears, whose tits are even sweeter—or, at any rate, newer? Or C, who knows how to move her ass in some special way I have never experienced; or D, or E, or F. I'm trying to be honest with you, Doctor—because with sex the human imagination runs to Z, and then beyond!

One could almost hear Lawrence cheering Portnoy's refusal, or wincing at his vulgarity, or both. Lawrence had, after all, offered a counterlist to Franklin's list, and his final responses would seem to have released Portnoy into his forest:

9. MODERATION

Beware of absolutes. There are many gods.

10. CLEANLINESS

Don't be too clean. It impoverishes the blood.

11. TRANQUILITY

The soul has many motions, many gods come
and go. Try and find your deepest issue, in every
confusion, and abide by that. Obey the man in
whom you recognize the Holy Ghost; command
when your honour comes to command.

12. CHASTITY

Never "use" venery at all. Follow your passional
impulse, if it be answered in the other being; but
never have any motive in mind, neither offspring
nor health nor even pleasure, nor even service.
Only know that "venery" is of the great gods. An
offering-up of yourself to the very great gods, the
dark ones, and nothing else.

13. HUMILITY

See all men and women according to the Holy
Ghost that is within them. Never yield before the
barren.

Roth told me that he had read Lawrence's essays on
American literature many years before writing *Portnoy's
Complaint*, though he could barely remember the essay on

Franklin, or confirm its influence—no more than pin Portnoy's sensibility directly on Flaubert, or Conrad, or James, or Freud. What's crucial here is that Lawrence's Franklin, like Portnoy's Mommy, presumed to suppress— to borrow a term from Franklin's physics—an "energy." Both failed to understand that matter *mattered* precisely because it embodied such energy. Human beings—again, Lawrence—don't just "grow potatoes or Chicagoes."

The danger Roth was implying, even in his farce, was that so much impacted energy could not be safely contained, especially if it were not acknowledged—a theme he didn't fully push until *The Plot Against America*. Lawrence, for his part, had implied much the same thing, ending his essay on Franklin anticipating, as few contemporaries did, and with a certain admiring ambivalence, how "the paddock" was sprouting the seeds of fascism: "Now is your chance, Europe. Now let Hell loose and get your own back, and paddle your own canoe on a new sea, while clever America lies on her muck-heaps of gold, strangled in her own barbed wire of shalt-not ideals and shalt-not moralisms . . ."

Nor is the danger ever overcome. Not long ago, the *New York Times* published a story about how an Alabama boy, Omar Hammami, had become a Somali jihadist. The author of the piece, a journalist by the name of Andrea

Elliott, writes that she could not understand what had happened:

> On a warm, cloudy day in the fall of 1999, the town of Daphne, Ala., stirred to life. The high-school band came pounding down Main Street, past the post office and the library and Christ the King Church. Trumpeters in gold-tasseled coats tipped their horns to the sky, heralding the arrival of teenage demigods. The star quarterback and his teammates came first in the parade, followed by the homecoming queen and her court. Behind them, on a float bearing leaders of the student government, a giddy mop-haired kid tossed candy to the crowd.
>
> Omar Hammami had every right to flash his magnetic smile. He had just been elected president of his sophomore class. He was dating a luminous blonde, one of the most sought-after girls in school. He was a star in the gifted-student program, with visions of becoming a surgeon. For a 15-year-old, he had remarkable charisma.
>
> Despite the name he acquired from his father, an immigrant from Syria, Hammami was every bit as Alabaman as his mother, a warm, plain-spoken woman who sprinkles her conversation with blandishments

like "sugar" and "darlin'." Brought up a Southern Baptist, Omar went to Bible camp as a boy and sang "Away in a Manger" on Christmas Eve. As a teenager, his passions veered between Shakespeare and Kurt Cobain, soccer and Nintendo. In the thick of his adolescence, he was fearless, raucously funny, rebellious, contrarian. "It felt cool just to be with him," his best friend at the time, Trey Gunter, said recently. "You knew he was going to be a leader."[6]

True enough, moving from a luminous blonde to Somali Jihadism may be more or less inexplicable. But the idea that band, church, grades, et cetera—when served up by Bible camp, and a home full of "sugar and darlin'"—might be a part of the explanation seems not to have crossed Ms. Elliott's mind. "I am a moral animal," Lawrence said; "but I am not a moral machine. I don't work with a little set of handles or levers." The soul is "a dark forest," he (and, indeed, Shakespeare and Kurt Cobain) told us; "my known self will never be more than a little clearing in the forest."

The question is—so Roth challenged his Bard students—will the repellent be allowed human status, or does it disqualify you from claiming human status?

But if it disqualifies you, it disqualifies others as well. So what are we going to do with all these repellent, radically impure people? If we don't admit that they are human too, and what and who is human?

Roth, obviously warming to the subject, defaults to capital letters:

RADICAL IMPURITY. IT'S SO SHAMING. AND YET SO REAL, SO PRESENT. SO PERVASIVE. THE DISGUSTING IS EVERY-WHERE. IT'S NOT JUST IN "THEM" — IT'S IN US. THAT'S THE WE THAT IS INESCAPABLE. (JEWS TOO. MEN TOO. WOMEN TOO.)

He then added in his own hand, underlining for emphasis, "I believe the Catholics call it *original sin.*"

Not coincidentally, any number of feminist writers have combed through *Portnoy's Complaint* and found something repellent in every punctuation mark. Roth has since been accused of writing about women unsympathetically, reducing them to objects, or as instruments of male pleasure. Vivian Gornick would famously write that Roth (along with Bellow and Mailer, actually) "hated women." Even Roth's great friend Hermione Lee, interviewing him in the *Paris Review* in 1984, put the matter delicately: "But supposing I say to you that nearly all the women in the books are there to obstruct, or to help, or to console the male characters. There's the woman who cooks and consoles and is sane and calming, or the other kind of woman, the dangerous maniac, the obstructor." (Roth answered, affectionately: "Let's face it, some women who are sane also happen to know how to cook. So do some of the dangerous maniacs. Let's leave out the sin of cooking.")

It was no use to protest, Roth seemed to understand (protesting to Lee), that a male writer who writes where he finds his material will write from the vantage point of male sexuality, much the same way an American Jew will write about American Jews and not American Koreans. Besides, he told her, many men find themselves in a situation "where having found the calm and consoling woman he can live with, a woman of *numerous* qualities, he then finds his desire for her perversely seeping away, and realizes that unless this involuntary diminution of passion can be arrested, he'll become alienated from the best thing in his life. Doesn't that happen either? From what I hear this damn seeping away of desire happens all the time and is extremely distressing to the people involved."

As for *Portnoy's Complaint*, a great many women (that is, "WOMEN TOO") read the novel with the same sense of liberation that men did; indeed, many had written Roth to offer thanks (and more). One might add that Portnoy does not objectify women until after he has objectified himself; that original sin means ubiquitous desire; that misanthropy is not misogyny, except by implication. Could

Erica Jong have sold 20 million copies of *Fear of Flying* had Portnoy not opened his big *piske* first? And what men in Grace Paley's wonderful stories come out remotely as shrewd or whole as her women? Paley once told me that she didn't trust women who refuse to read Roth. (I might add that, next to Mickey Sabbath's meltdown in *Sabbath's Theater*, Catharine MacKinnon's descriptions of male sexual aggression seem a tad impressionistic; Harold Bloom thinks of *Sabbath's Theater*, wisely, as *Portnoy's Complaint* in its tragic mode.)

A final point about Portnoy as satirist. I noted before how disquieting the sixties were, but that is a half-truth. *Portnoy's Complaint* would have been barely imaginable had America not also been comfortably rich. Nikita Khrushchev had banged his shoe at the United Nations and shown off the peoples' refrigerators to Vice President Nixon in Moscow. But it was members of the American middle class who were living the charmed lives. American corporations supplied the Western world with most everything it needed, even as the U.S. military acted to define the earth's perimeters. Then John Glenn went into orbit around it. From the United Auto Workers in Michigan to new residents of Los Angeles, Americans expected a stable life: a university degree for those who wanted it, two cars even for those who dropped out of high school to "go to work."

The educated liberalism that had triumphed over fascism found its voice on the CBS Evening News—Charles Collingwood at the White House, Richard C. Hottelet at the United Nations—correspondents who now descended, appalled, on Selma, Alabama. For young people, homes were launching pads, not just safe harbors. If Portnoy did not imagine himself comfortable, could he imagine ambition in all its torturing purity?

"You see, I just can't stop! Or tie myself to any *one*," Portnoy exclaims. You could not quite imagine him saying this while standing in a breadline, or sitting by the radio listening to FDR's reassurances after Pearl Harbor. Lawrence insisted he was "a forest," not "a neat garden." That's easier to say when the war to end all wars is over and, for now at least, the forest is not a place where you will be taken out and shot. Adam Gopnik put the matter powerfully in an essay about Voltaire's garden: "It is not so much the establishment of a garden but the ownership of a gate that moves people from liking a society based on favors to one based on rights. Enclosing his garden broadened Voltaire's circle of compassion. When people were dragged from *their* gardens to be tortured and killed in the name of faith, he began to take it, as they say, personally."

If *Portnoy's Complaint* could be said to have a fault, then, it is our hero's utter lack of morbidity. He is in his thirties, old enough to know better. Oh, Portnoy might allude to anticipated loss, the possible death of his father, say, but this has the cushioned feel of a still-little boy not *really* understanding that his father will lie gray and stiff and (can one even imagine this?) oblivious before his eyes. This kind of knowledge, Portnoy reassures himself, is in Spielvogel's realm, not his. ("And whether what I hear I hear out of compassion for him, out of my agony over the inevitability of this horrific occurrence, his death, or out of my eager anticipation of that event, is also something else again. But this of course you understand, this of course is your bread and butter.")

Shocking the bourgeois, in this sense, seems like poking a friendly giant. Sexually, politically, *institutionally*, Portnoy pushes against constraints, but he seems to expect Locke's comfortable state of nature, where property and decency still prevail—not Hobbes's war of all against all, where brutes slice into the chests of enemies. Everything is couched in Portnoy's knowing irony, but he knows even less than he thinks he does. Portnoy's young, defeated neighbor, Ronald Nimkin—so Portnoy tells us—leaves a suicide note: "Mrs. Blumenthal called. Please bring your mah-jongg rules to the game tonight." This is one of those laugh-out-loud moments, a perfect joke against Mrs. Nimkin's home, even if you suppose Portnoy is making the story up for Spielvogel or embellishing some facts for effect. But, actually, the story has only a slightly different timbre than the unfunny story of Cousin Heshie, who is beaten into submission by his father, gives up his shikse girlfriend, and then dies "in the war." In both cases, the deaths are used mainly to bring proof against the suffocating smallness of the family circle ("At least he didn't leave you with *goyische* children . . ."). It is proof of the domestic brutality that is everywhere, the flip-side of original sin, what Roth would later call in *The Human Stain* the "persecuting spirit."

Portnoy's Complaint gives us no view from the parents in the family drama, though Portnoy purports, as young sons and daughters do, to psyche-out his parents. Portnoy can no more contemplate death (or contemplate how no one truly can) than contemplate another Great Depression. Death is really a comic way of upping the ante— a way of taking Mrs. Nimkin's pedestrian faults to mythic levels, or carrying curiosity to ultimate places. Portnoy's parents' talk of death is—so he thinks—just a way of inducing guilt and making commands stick. There is, in *Portnoy's Complaint*, a great deal of parental sweetness; without this, the complaints would not be painful and self-subverting. But there is no miracle of birth, no mystery to physical life—none of William James's sickness of the soul, either. Dying seems a threat as distant as defeated Nazis beyond the ocean. If, as in *Nemesis*, the Portnoys were living through a polio epidemic, Sophie's plea, "Alex, don't flush!" would sound quite different, would it not?

Portnoy, in short, doesn't really know, or pretends that he doesn't care, about pains that are not just grievances. Those characters are saved for Roth's next big novels. Nor is the pursuit of B and C even mildly burdened by recognition of A's mortality. Custodians of well-being come to us as the annoying voice on the other side of the bathroom door; there is virtually none of the panic a mother might plausibly feel for the very life of her child; or at least her panic is presented as an inherently exaggerated thing, contributing to Portnoy's sense of fecklessness.

But then, this absence of what is morbid and parental is a *good* fault in a novel formed around a psychoanalytic confession. And it adds strongly to the book's enigma. If Portnoy *is* old enough to know better he is young enough not to care. He is not dwelling on the end. He is going to a shrink for a mid-course correction. Portnoy might have known in principle, if only by watching the lovers at Rick's Café on the big screen, that the problems of little people don't amount to a hill of beans in this crazy world. But really, what if your problem is still amounting to a hill of beans to yourself?

It all feels so youthful and American, this self-centeredness, this hypothetical sense of loss, and this talk of tragedy that rolls away from consciousness like images of a Hollywood massacre at the post-theater ice-cream parlor. Even that long, gloomy passage about the staleness of sex in marriage, which registers a kind of unsettling gravitas, gives us no more than doublethink. I defy any married person to read *Portnoy's Complaint*, at any time of life, and not suddenly find oneself anxiously reviewing all the reasons for staying married; wondering if the reasons are just self-deception, or some deeper wisdom—wondering, and then cutting the tomatoes for lunch and suppressing the questions. Is it the syrups of sex that are icky, really, or the dodges of devotion?

Then again, if Portnoy is right about married love, what to make of Grace Paley's garden?

> that's my old man across the yard
> he's talking to the meter reader
> he's telling him the world's sad story
> how electricity is oil or uranium
> and so forth I tell my grandson
> run over to your grandpa ask him
> to sit beside me for a minute I
> am suddenly exhausted by my desire
> to kiss his sweet explaining lips.[7]

Books that push us into serious ruminations about our loyalties—we who have a property in our own persons—

are going to stay around, even if they don't become own-
ers' manuals. *Portnoy's Complaint* quickly established itself
as one such book. How, unless you think you *will* live forever, can you want and *want!* like a real American, as if
there is nothing to lose? What better proof of the repellent than a man who thinks he should have mastered self-
control—has braced himself with law and reason and an
unrivaled knowledge of suffering—and then sets himself
up for suffering in an entirely unexpected way? This brings
us back, more carefully this time, to American Jews.

CHAPTER THREE

"The Best Kind"

Portnoy as the Object of Satire

If Portnoy could be said to have had a first foil—one he could admit to, and we could never forget laughing about bashfully and in sympathy—it was the family rabbi, Rabbi Warshaw, "a fat, pompous, impatient fraud, with an absolutely grotesque superiority complex, a character out of Dickens is what he is . . ." Our fourteen-year-old hero is just finding his stride:

> This is a man who somewhere along the line got the idea that the basic unit of meaning in the English language is the syllable. So no word he pronounces has less than three of them, not even the word *God* . . . "I-a wan-tt to-a wel-come-a you-ew tooo thee sy-no-gawg-a." Oh God, oh Guh-ah-duh, if you're up there

shining down your countenance, why not spare us from here on out the enunciation of the rabbis! Why not spare us the rabbis themselves! Look, why not spare us religion, if only in the name of our human dignity! Good Christ, Mother, the whole world knows already, so why don't you? *Religion is the opiate of the people!* And if believing that makes me a fourteen-year-old Communist, then that's what I am, *and I'm proud of it!* . . . Because I am sick and tired of *goyische* this and *goyische* that! If it's bad it's the *goyim*, if it's good it's the Jews! . . . The very first distinction I learned from you, I'm sure, was not night and day, or hot and cold, but *goyische* and Jewish!

The "Jewish Blues" begin. It is hard to find a page of *Portnoy's Complaint* in which the Jewish family, and the larger Jewish world it is stewing in, are not on Portnoy's mind. Even after Portnoy is all but exhausted by doubts and affection, even after he is done with parents and The Monkey and shikses and advancing civil rights, he finds himself in Israel, of all places, where his confidence collapses and his sexual desire fizzles. Yet his rage is never quelled and Jews remain in his sights.

He picks up a lovely young soldier and tries taking her to bed. He finds himself impotent, apparently, for the first time. So he doubles down, unleashing residual hysterical energy against Israel's historical force. After fumbling around the country a little more, he meets the formidable Naomi, a Zionist dish who had come from America (and who, conveniently for Spielvogel, reminds him vaguely of his mother), whom Portnoy finally gets to his room. He fantasizes about forcing himself on her, or forcing himself into marriage with her, while she tries to instruct him in the ways of the world:

> "The way [so says Naomi] you disapprove of your
> life! Why do you do that? It is of no value for a man
> to disapprove of his life the way that you do. You
> seem to take some special pleasure, some pride, in
> making yourself the butt of your own peculiar sense
> of humor. I don't believe you actually want to improve
> your life. Everything you say is somehow always
> twisted, some way or another, to come out 'funny.'
> All day long the same thing. In some little way or
> other, everything is ironical, or self-deprecating . . ."
> "Oh, I don't know," I said, "self-deprecation is,
> after all, a classic form of Jewish humor."
> "Not Jewish humor! No! *Ghetto* humor."
> Not much love in that remark, I'll tell you. By
> dawn I had been made to understand that I was the
> epitome of what was most shameful in "the culture
> of the Diaspora." Those centuries and centuries of

homelessness had produced just such disagreeable men as myself—frightened, defensive, self-deprecating, unmanned and corrupted by life in the gentile world . . .

When she finished I said, "Wonderful. Now let's fuck . . ."

"Mr. Portnoy," she said, raising her knapsack from the floor, "you are nothing but a self-hating Jew."

"Ah, but Naomi, maybe that's the best kind."

Passages like this were bound to offend Jews, and especially Jews no longer charmed by the self-deprecating humor of *Yiddishkeit*. So consider the context and some offending passages more broadly:

Here are early midlife confessions of an eloquent, caustic, self-described neurotic; a self-obsessed Jew, convinced his torments are instructive, pouring out his life to a psychoanalytic ear. There is, on his landscape, a compelling figure: a strong, invasive, anxiety-plagued, supposedly self-sacrificing, but actually self-aggrandizing, mother. He once adored her which is why he now hates her—let's say she has a problem with boundaries. On the other hand, there is his feckless, indulgent, relentless, responsible, business-whipped father, physically weak, unlucky, blocked—home but not quite around. Thoughts of Mommy and Daddy are of a piece with febrile sexual fantasies, which mature (if that's the word for it) into a fierce pursuit of Gentile women, whose attributed *un*selfcon-sciousness, apparent (but deceptive) air of freedom, com-plete a kind of sexual loop. Women start out irresistible, then turn human, then needy, then frantic—Helena licks your neck, only to become an albatross around it.

Eventually, our hero determines he must be a man. He moves from Mommy to action. He gives himself to "en-lightenment," to becoming worthy of the *goy*. Then he dreams a superseding dream, that of finding salvation of sorts among Zionist pioneers or a Hebrew fuck, a dream that yields to yet another sad discovery: that he can never surrender to Jewish "claustrophilia." Indeed, he discovers that Hebrews, the stolid residents of the land of Israel, have lost touch with the Jews' instinctive self-criticism. The sideshow brings us that other character, the nice Jewish girl—filled with compassion for the forsaken peo-ple, their good works, with good-hearted defenses against the Jews' enemies—a woman who projects the kind of love in which recklessness has been banished and desire feels vaguely incestuous. In fact, all Jewish women come to seem this way:

> Their flesh [Doctor!] had lost its innocence from birth. . . . [S]ome acrid spice of their intellect perme-ated the very pores of their bodies . . . knowingness expanded over the nervous surface of their skin,

destroyed their capacity for self-forgetfulness. They were saturated with the long experience of the race which lingered in their eyes and on their skin like the heat of the former occupant in a chair.

Actually, this last passage is not the forlorn Portnoy speaking to Spielvogel about, say, his soldierette with whom he flamed out. The narrator is Joseph, the hero of Arthur Koestler's 1946 novel, *Thieves in the Night*, explaining why he found himself so lonely in the kibbutzim of pre-state Palestine. (Okay, I added [Doctor!] to throw you off.) Furthermore, the memories here were Koestler's —mother, father, "Helena"—addressed to readers whose sensibilities were, he supposed, like those of a "nimble-witted psychoanalyst." They were published in Koestler's best-selling memoir, *Arrow in the Blue*, in 1952. Oh, and "claustrophilia" was Koestler's word, too, which he coined in his 1949 report from Israel, *Promise and Fulfillment*, after a discussion with national orthodox politicians.

All of which raises a question. If Koestler's self-advertised neurosis regarding mothers, sex—hence, he thought, Jews—was in the public realm fully seventeen years before *Portnoy's Complaint*, why did Roth's book prompt such grievances in 1969, while Koestler's works, published serially over much of the previous generation, caused hardly a stir? Koestler was no shrinking violet. When he wrote his memoirs he was arguably the most famous writer in the world. By 1947, his great novel *Darkness at Noon* had sold more copies in Europe than any novel in history: some say the publication of its French edition, *Le Zéro et l'infini*, was single-handedly responsible for preventing the Communists from winning the election of 1946.

I have already suggested something of an answer. It is that the timing and nature of Portnoy's rhetoric suggested a powerful satire of bourgeois constraints: Roth—so the *best* of his Jewish critics thought—turned his arsenal on Jewish sexuality to mock the middle class, that is, just when Jews had finally joined it and its foibles seemed grounds for a "generation gap." So it was hard to see that Roth was actually mocking Portnoy most of all. Few really took seriously what Roth told Plimpton from the start, that Portnoy's exaggerations, resentments, obscenities, and desires were hardly there to be emulated—that the greatest enticement of *Portnoy's Complaint* was seeing how much Portnoy flies in the face of *his own* normalizing passion and becomes an object of his own spite.

Koestler's readers, unlike Roth's, presumably, had been left with no doubt that Koestler's repressed-and-salacious-

Jew confessions were meant to be those of a young man who had finally come to maturity, a point I made earlier about Augustine's *Confessions*. Okay, Koestler had his Jewish critics, especially when it came to his skeptical view of the Diaspora, his impatience with Judaism, a prejudice he had reinforced working for his erstwhile hero, the Revisionist Zionist leader Jabotinsky. But in his sexual life —anyway, before later accusations of rape surfaced— Koestler was thought simply to be exhibiting youthful insecurities, like those that had brought him to Marxist method. One could not be sure that the hero of *Portnoy's Complaint* regrets anything.

Koestler once said that the Cold War was the confrontation between the Big Lie and a half-truth. If the Lie in American life during Roth's childhood had been that Jews were vulgar, tribal, and sly, or, in his young adulthood, that they were the embodiment of bourgeois goodness, then Portnoy's half-truth was that they were Alex and Sophie and Rabbi Warshaw and Naomi. Koestler yearned for Helena. But goddesses failed him clearly because of his own neurosis, not theirs. It is not so clear with Portnoy. He fantasizes explaining his name to Thereal McCoy at the skating rink ("Portnoy, yes, it's an old French name, a corruption of porte-noire, meaning black door or gate . . ."), and he seems justifiably ashamed of his schnoz and manners, determined to win the girl with her plum pudding (whatever that may be), and her one-family house with a banister and a staircase, and parents who are tranquil and patient and *dignified,* and also a big brother Billy who knows how to take motors apart and says "Much obliged," and isn't afraid of anything physical, and oh the way she'll cuddle next to me on the sofa in her Angora sweater with her legs pulled back up beneath her tartan skirt, and the way she'll turn at the doorway and say to me, "And thank you ever so much for such a wonderful wonderful evening," and then this amazing creature—to whom no one has ever said *"Shah!"* or "I only hope your children will do the same to you someday!"—this perfect, perfect-stranger, who is as smooth and shiny and cool as custard, will kiss me—raising up one shapely calf behind her—and my nose and my name will have become as nothing.

Roth, unlike Koestler, finally, sailed into a perfect storm of Jewish literary power. Nineteen sixty-nine was the heyday of Jewish intellectuals centered in New York. It corresponded, coincidentally, with the heyday of Jewish military power, the heady aftermath of the Six Day War. The writer Nicholas Lemann has described the New York Jewish intellectuals of the time as "the American Bloomsbury"—Columbia, CUNY, the magazines, the publishing houses, the "media." And they were mostly Jews: Philip Rahv, William Phillips, Clement Greenberg, Harold Rosenberg, Meyer Shapiro, Sidney Hook, the Trillings, the Bells, Bellow, Malamud, Kazin, Kristol, Podhoretz, Howe, the Epsteins, Susan Sontag, Robert Silvers —need I continue? There was, especially after the 1967 war, a growing interest in American Jewish identity, and Portnoy seemed almost calculated to force very articulate people into camps.

Isaac Bashevis Singer had told the *Paris Review* in the fall of 1968, just before *Portnoy's Complaint* was published: "To me there are only Yiddish writers, Hebrew writers, English writers, Spanish writers. The whole idea of a Jewish writer, or a Catholic writer, is kind of far-fetched to me." Young Roth no doubt concurred (though he once asked me if "far-fetched" was not itself Yiddish). And a novel expressing a tortured Jewish sensibility of Portnoy's sort might well have been the ideal fiction for the New York intellectuals, people like Kazin—Americans for whom Jewishness was more conundrum than identity.

By the end of the sixties, however, there was a kind of turmoil, a changing of the guard, in the Jewish intelligentsia. Community leaders began insisting on the "centrality" of Israel for Jewish life. They pointed to a valiant Israeli democracy and shrugged off the occupation of the

West Bank, which they assumed would be temporary. The preeminent Jewish organizations, local philanthropic federations, began to devote as much as half of their funds to Israel (which is still more or less true). They rallied to support Israeli diplomacy during exchanges of fire on the Suez Canal, terrorist attacks, and, most horribly, the 1973 war. Jewish intellectuals, mostly on the academic left, did not exactly let themselves be led by such organizations, but they often spoke in synagogues, raised money from philanthropists, and made common cause with Jewish big-shots in Democratic Party politics.

On the erstwhile left, *Commentary* magazine was already showing signs of the neoconservatism that would colonize it more completely over the next decade. The Six Day War in 1967 was a watershed; Jews everywhere were swept up by the victory, and faith in the justice of Jewish armed power helped, subtly, to shape Jewish attitudes toward American politics and foreign policy. In the back of more and more American Jewish minds was the need to reverse the U.S. State Department's traditional tilt toward the Arab oil regimes, beginning with the otherwise idolized George Marshall and George Kennan. Many Jews were drawn to political allies of Senator Henry "Scoop" Jackson of Washington, who argued, flatly, that Israel was to be promoted as America's key regional ally against the Soviets. Israeli self-defense seemed an inspiration to ethnic realpolitik in America: should not Jews confront the violence against them in U.S. cities, like the confrontation in 1968 between Jewish teachers and black parents demanding community control of schools in Brooklyn's Ocean Hill–Brownsville?

The seeds for an agonistic view of American Jewish power were evident as early as 1964—the year Jews voted 9 to 1 for Lyndon Johnson over Barry Goldwater. The previous year, *Commentary* editor Norman Podhoretz had written his notorious article "My Negro Problem—and Ours." Podhoretz acknowledged how the civil rights movement was cardinal for Jews, but that was precisely his "problem." He implied that Jews were soft but had made it; that their support for the economic empowerment of black toughs ("who act as though they have nothing to lose") was if not self-destructive then at least disingenuous. Why, his magazine asked, should Jews earn like Episcopalians and vote like Puerto Ricans? The fact that certain black militants came to rationalize anti-Semitism as a form of rage against ghetto storekeepers seemed to make his point. For—dare one say it?—an emerging Jewish right, there was a universal Jewish vulnerability that required a universal Jewish toughness. It was as if there was an ongoing referendum on the virtue of Jewish power, whose implicit foils were Great Society initiatives at home and United Nations' resolutions abroad. This was not going to be a sensibility that could digest either Portnoy's versions of his family or, worse, his *schlemiel* version of himself.

Even on the recalcitrant left, the crowd's wisdom was inclined to receive the book skeptically. As the anti-war movement grew into "radical" politics, Jewish intellectuals such as Howe, Bell, and Nathan Glazer, people who as young men had prided themselves on resisting Soviet Communism while holding to Marxian insights, now positioned themselves by the degrees to which their "socialism" had been shaken off or clung to. (Howe would write, ironizing religious speech: "Socialism is the name of our desire.") Lines, and identities, hardened as the New Left grabbed much of the airspace. Veteran socialists like Howe and other founders of *Dissent* magazine—Stanley Plastrik, Lewis Coser—suddenly found themselves on the defensive. When a New Left student leader named Cohen asked by what right Howe still called himself a radical, Howe responded, incensed, "Cohen, you know what you're going to end up as—a dentist! And I'll be a radical after you start pulling teeth." (Actually, Cohen *did* become a dentist.)

The bone of contention was whether "self-realization" was best understood in political economic or psychological ways—in a nutshell, whether revolutions are incubated in the workplace or in bed, which is not so obvious when you think about it. As Mark Schechner put it, people of the left both reflected and resisted the movement from the "politics of social redemption" to the "politics of self-renewal," "Socialism to Therapy." For older radicals, to embrace Freud's questions seemed a kind of abandonment of Marx, who of course *should* have been abandoned, but not like *that*. Howe summed up his reservations about the New Left in *A Margin of Hope*: "We bore marks of 'corrosion and distrust' . . . they looked forward to clusterings of fraternity. . . . We had pulled ourselves out of an immigrant working class, an experience not likely to induce romantic views about the poor; they, children of warm liberals and cooled radicals, were hoping to find a way into the lives and wisdom of the oppressed."[1]

It was within this American pond that the Jewish question bubbled to the surface, where *Portnoy's Complaint* created unusual ripples. What exactly *were* the psychological propensities that made one, if not leftist, then "alienated"? Here is where Howe, dredging, found an admirable, decaying Judaism:

> We knew we were Jews. We had no choice but to remain Jews, except perhaps through devices too humiliating to consider. We took an acute private

pleasure, through jokes and asides, in those aspects
of intellectuality that bore the marks of Jewishness:
quickness, skepticism, questioning. But we had no
taste for and little interest in Judaism as religion. We
refused to acknowledge ourselves as part of an American Jewish community encompassing all classes and
opinions, since we claimed that the inner divisions of
social interest and political opinion among the Jews
remained decisive.[2]

Howe was by now translating Yiddish stories and thinking about a big history of American Jews, the book that
would become his only best-seller, *World of Our Fathers.*
Revealingly, Kazin's first book, a 1942 study of modern
American writers, was called *On Native Grounds;* its five-
page introduction uses the possessive pronoun "our" (that
is, American) twenty-seven times. But his 1978 memoir
was unabashedly titled *New York Jew.* My wife, the Hebrew University critic Sidra DeKoven Ezrahi, put it this
way: "The unharnessed generation that came of age in
the late 1930s and 1940s, that inherited a repressed tradition, a cultural amnesia, succeeded in encoding in the
language of alienation what had already become in fact
a profound claim to being-at-home."[3] The 1967 war
also increased fascination with Jewish solidarity. If New
York intellectuals survived the ideological rifts of a post-

Communist time, their desire for "the clusterings of fraternity" was now focused largely on a shared Jewish pedi-
gree with the Labor Zionist heroes and writers they met
in Jerusalem. Besides, the Six Day War endowed Jewish
toughness with a kind of glamour, and some of the New
York intellectuals were happy to feel their Jewish "aspects"
less apologetically.

A portent of divided reactions to self-criticism and its
limits had flared up five years before over Hannah Arendt's *Eichmann in Jerusalem*. Arendt, covering the trial of
Adolf Eichmann for the *New Yorker*, had explored various
tragic episodes in which the Nazi death bureaucracy made
use of the discipline, records, and access of Jewish Coun-
cils in Europe, especially in Hungary. On its face, Arendt
seemed to be implying some sort of complicity—which,
in fairness, she did not—and that Nazis like Eichmann
were more bureaucrat than devil. This view seemed consistent with her grim (and less controversial) view of
totalitarianism—namely, that the bureaucracies of the
modern state were incipiently devilish in the way they
reduced people to digits. Many New York Jewish intellectuals, including Howe, accused Arendt of a lack of
moral spine. Presumably, Arendt was asking to judge certain Jewish victims more harshly and certain Nazis with
what appeared to be more empathy.

■

Portnoy's Complaint was therefore a natural target for neoconservatives and a natural test for "cooled radicals." Portnoy, or Roth, or whoever, *was* clearly being cavalier about the danger of anti-Semitism. What could be worse than a fictional hero indifferent to both socialism and the socialism of fools? Look at how the world shrugged when Nasser and the rest threatened to throw Israelis into the sea! Look at how black parents in Brooklyn, forgetting Jewish support for civil rights, turned on Jewish teachers! Look at how SNCC turned on Theodore Bikel and began courting Palestinians! Were Jewish humiliations really banished from America—could vigilance really be banished from Jewish identity?

Roth had already made a splash in 1960, after publishing his collection of stories, *Goodbye, Columbus.* He had written "Epstein," about a middle-aged Jewish adulterer, and "Defender of the Faith," in which a Jewish recruit tries (and fails) to play on tribal loyalties to get a Jewish veteran to let him out of combat. The young Roth had been denounced by rabbis in their pulpits. He received a letter that told him, in part, "you have done as much harm as all the organized anti-Semitic organizations have done to make people believe that all Jews are cheats, liars and connivers." Roth had been put on notice, in a way: a Jewish writer could go only so far in empowering a character to expose a Jewish family for garden-variety repression, hypocrisy, or bigotry against Gentiles. Nevertheless, Roth knew (what he told that Bard College class in 1999) that the dirtiest secret of *Portnoy's Complaint* was not masturbation but ordinary brutality; that a Jewish family's glossing over its own little cruelties was a building block of Portnoy's own farcical disaster—and that he, Portnoy, has the nerve to say so, at least in private to his analyst. The son took a shikse girlfriend and didn't want to give her up. The uncle goes to the girl and tells her that the young man has poison in his blood and that *she* should give *him* up. He gives her some money. In that instant there is something new and provocative; even in Clifford Odets's famous *Golden Boy* there was nothing this brutal.

Many Jews, even on the left, were not amused. They assumed that young Jews ought not to indulge their "quickness, skepticism," et cetera, *this* much. Okay, Jews were now Americans; they could take the veiled, gentle criticism of Arthur Miller's plays, or Sid Caesar's *Your Show of Shows*—even a Howl or two from Allen Ginsberg. But fictional Jews were expected to look more like Mr. Nazerman, the hero of the 1964 Hollywood blockbuster *The Pawnbroker*—a man haunted by persecution and grudgingly representing the Rights of Man. Jewish intellectuals had earned fraternity, especially now that anxiety in the face of historical anti-Semitism—not, surely, "Judaism as a religion"—was the *basis* of fraternity. The last thing to imply, certainly, was that Jews might themselves somehow be responsible for inciting Jew-hatred.

Roth had weathered the controversy surrounding the publication of *Goodbye, Columbus* in reasonably good spirits. Rather than angering New York Jewish intellectuals as a group, he had become the darling of some. His collection won a National Book Award for fiction. Howe had celebrated him. Yes, there were some hard moments with Philistines who called Roth out to do combat. In 1962, while still teaching in Iowa, he had accepted an invitation to speak at Yeshiva University, on a panel about "the crisis of conscience of minority writers"—a panel including Ralph Ellison, among others, whose landmark 1952 novel *Invisible Man* was itself now being criticized by certain black nationalists. The night was, Roth told David Remnick, a kind of slaughter, with question after question challenging the young writer—who was otherwise thrilled by the attention—to justify how his work would not have warmed the hearts of Nazis. Over and over Roth answered: "But we live in the *opposite* of Nazi Germany." He got nowhere. ("Finally, in about the eleventh round, when Ralph had the feeling I couldn't come out for the twelfth," Ellison said that he had himself gotten mail from black readers furious with him for having depicted incest in a black family. Ellison insisted on a writer's independence, that he was not just "a cog in the machinery of civil-rights legislation.") And after the evening had ended, Roth told friends, over a pastrami sandwich at the Stage Delicatessen, that he would never write about Jews again; indeed, his next two novels, *Letting Go* and *When She Was Good*, seemed tame, enWASPed, mannered, at least as compared with the stories of *Goodbye, Columbus*.

But Roth might as well have vowed to give up pastrami. Soon he went on the offensive, playing jujitsu with the criticism, writing defenses of his stories in Jewish magazines which, revealingly, were pleased to publish him. The most explicit apologia was his essay "Writing About Jews," which *Commentary* showcased in 1963:

> The issue is not knowledge of one's "people." At least, it is not a question of who has more historical data at his fingertips, or is more familiar with Jewish tradition, or which of us observes more customs and rituals. It is even possible, needless to say, to "know" a good deal about tradition, and to misunderstand what it is that tradition signifies. The story of Lou Epstein stands or falls not on how much I know about tradition but on how much I know and understand about Lou Epstein. Where the history of the Jewish people comes down in time and place to become the man

whom I called Epstein, that is where my knowledge must be sound.[4]

Indeed, as *Portnoy's Complaint* was taking shape in dinner-table shtick, the frictions in organized Jewish communities may have even provoked the book a little. Roth realized that in spite of Jewish criticism, or perhaps because of it, there was a vein to be mined. Finally, he thought—so he told me when we first met in 1974—*You wanna fight?*

Yet nothing in the controversy about *Goodbye, Columbus* really prepared Roth for the brawl he now provoked. Within months of publishing *Portnoy's Complaint*, Roth was angrily, publicly denounced. He had fomented anti-Semitism; he had shamed the tribe; he had degraded the foundations of the examined life. Perhaps the most powerful reaction was from the Hebrew University historian and guru of *Bildung*, Gershom Scholem, whose work on the fanatic weirdness of Jewish messianists was now legendary, and whose pen was still warm from chastising Hannah Arendt for her alleged lack of "love of the people of Israel." In the elite Hebrew daily *Haaretz*, Scholem described Alexander Portnoy as "the loathsome figure whom the anti-Semites have conjured in their imagination and portrayed in their literature. . . . This is the book for which all anti-Semites have been praying. . . . We [Jews]

will pay the price, not the author who revels in obscenities." He continued:

> The fact is that the hero of a best-seller, avidly ac-
> quired by the public, proclaimed (and lives his procla-
> mation) that his behavior is shaped by a single lust
> which becomes the slogan of his life: to get "*shikse
> cunt.*" . . . I daresay that with the next turn of history,
> not long to be delayed, this book will make all of us
> [Jews] defendants at court. . . . This book will be
> quoted to us—and how it will be quoted! They will
> say to us: Here you have the testimony from one of
> your own artists . . . an authentic Jewish witness. . . .
> I wonder what price *k'lal yisrael* [the world Jewish
> community]—and there is such an entity in the eyes
> of the Gentiles—is going to pay for this book. Woe
> to us on that day of reckoning![5]

Other Jewish critics joined in the chorus. Marie Syrkin,
the political essayist (and biographer of her socialist-
Zionist theorist father, Nachman Syrkin), conceded that
"Roth is a gifted mimic with a superb ear for the intona-
tions of dialogue." Nonetheless, Roth had written an anti-
Semitic novel, one with "Julius Streicher's satanic Jewboy
lusting after Aryan maidens . . ." *Commentary* weighed
in. Peter Shaw, an editor, observed that "Roth's insistence
that he is a friend to the Jews can only theoretically be

squared with the loathing for them that he displays in his work." The real message of the novel, Shaw writes, is not to sweep away anti-Semitism, but to transcend being Jewish. Roth's art will not do the Jews any more damage than "other specious advice they have received from time to time"; even if he has not been bad *for* the Jews, Roth has "decidedly been bad *to* them."

Curiously, none of these reviewers took account of the way Roth had written Portnoy a foil as tough as any of them: his sane, dull big sister Hannah, whose brassiere had sent him into ecstasy, but who defends the endless cautions of their parents—cleanliness over *shmutz*, responsibility over recklessness, Jews over *goyim*—as reasonable in a way readers could hardly gainsay.

"It is coming out of my ears already"—so Portnoy remembers being fourteen years old and regaling Hannah, refusing to go to synagogue—"the saga of the suffering Jews! Do me a favor, my people, and stick your suffering heritage up your suffering ass—*I happen also to be a human being!*" Which only sets up Hannah to cut him down:

> Dead. Gassed, or shot [Hannah says], or incinerated, or butchered, or buried alive. Do you know that? And you could have screamed all you wanted that you were not a Jew, that you were a human being and had nothing whatever to do with their stupid

suffering heritage, and still you would have been taken away to be disposed of. You would be dead, and I would be dead, and

But that isn't what I'm talking about!

And your mother and your father would be dead.

But why are you taking their side!

I'm not taking anybody's side, she says. I'm only telling you he's not such an ignorant person as you think.

And she isn't either, I suppose! I suppose the Nazis make everything she says and does smart and brilliant too! I suppose the Nazis are an excuse for everything that happens in this house!

Oh, I don't know, says my sister, maybe, maybe they are, and now she begins to cry too, and how monstrous I feel, for she sheds her tears for six million, or so I think, while I shed mine only for myself. Or so I think.

Or so I think. As if young Portnoy doesn't *know* about Nazis. As if he doesn't know that he really *doesn't* know about Nazis. As if his parents really know about Nazis— or *would* know, in their middle-class home, even after *The Diary of Anne Frank* or reading accounts of the Eichmann trial. There is a moral fatuousness here, which Portnoy at times attacks and, at other times, fears he exemplifies.

Nevertheless, Kingsley Amis, writing probably the most leaden of the novel's negative reviews, continued *Commentary*'s line in *Harper's*, in a piece commissioned by then executive editor Midge Decter (not coincidentally, the wife of *Commentary*'s editor, Norman Podhoretz). Amis complained about how bathetic *schlemiel* Jewish humor is ("it conceals, or fails to conceal, a ruefulness, a reflectiveness, a sense of resignation"), how incoherent Roth was in putting together this "autobiographical fiction," and how "provincial" Roth was in thinking that goyim were different from his fictionalized parents. "In Western society, and probably in a lot of other societies, past and present"— Amis is apparently struggling through his scotch for *le seul mot juste*—"people constantly try to straitjacket their children to be as they want, use guilt feelings on them, insist on being told everything they do . . . ," and so on in this vein. Amis further speculates that if Roth is right— that Jewish mothers are indeed "unbearable"—this might have "something to do with the position of women in Jewish society."

All of which opened the door for Diana Trilling, the wife of Podhoretz's mentor, Lionel Trilling, to write a longer piece for *Harper's* later that summer. She was concerned less with Roth's Streicher-like attacks on Jewish men than his attacks on Jewish mothers who, presumably, artfully engendered guilt and thus allegedly confounded the sexuality upon which happiness depended. Indifferent to how Portnoy's rants against himself *agreed* with her skepticism, she worried that the trashing of guilt undermined the very pillars of (what only a Trilling could call) "the whole modern human condition." Mr. Roth, she writes, as the "child of an indiscriminative mass society, achieves his effects by the broadest possible strokes."

> The force of contemporary culture presses us toward Mr. Roth's "position." And a "position" the author of *Portnoy's Complaint* is indeed fortifying: his book is farce with a thesis. . . . It is guilt that made Portnoy the athletic and ingenious masturbator that Mr. Roth shows him to have been in his boyhood, and it is guilt that makes him impotent with all except Gentile girls when he comes to manhood. . . . The prime purveyor of this guilt is, we see, his Jewish mother, who has ladled out injunction and precept. . . . In the view of Mr. Roth, guilt is only and always an alien substance in the human composition, introduced for the destruction of our joy and the perpetuation of old sorrows. . . . And this is of course why the Jewish condition, so supremely guilt laden, is now thought to offer literature its best material for describing the whole modern human condition—the alienated Jew is our most cogent instance of alienated modern man.[6]

The initial attacks did not much shake Roth's equanimity. But who could really stand an onslaught from critics who, whatever the unfairness of their views, seemed to give everybody at the lunch counter the right to wink at you with an intimacy that slides past reverence into condescension? *Of course* Roth's book gives us a hero venting in a pathetic, deterministic, self-absorbed rhetoric. Did it not dawn on Mrs. Trilling—or Amis, Syrkin, Scholem, and the rest—that this was precisely the author's intention? Besides, what exactly was that phrase "indiscriminative mass society" supposed to mean? It is one thing to claim that Jews became symbols of alienation—half-conscious custodians of a tradition of exile and idol-breaking. Or to claim, as David Riesman had, that one could be lonely in an American crowd. It was quite another thing to assume that Americans, or at least Americans outside of New York, were some "indiscriminative mass." Was Trilling's phrase evidence for the very corrupting smugness she was trying to pin on the author of *Portnoy's Complaint*?

"I once thought," Roth told radio host Christopher Lydon, recalling these early years as a novelist, "that the score would be University of Chicago 22, popular culture 6." Where were the reviewers, he now asked himself, who did not take literature so literally and superficially? Roth wrote a long letter in response to Trilling's article—

and then he slept on it. He never mailed it to *Harper's*, wisely perhaps, but he did eventually publish it in *Reading Myself and Others*, and it is among the most revealing and exasperated of his responses.

What multitudes of experience are encompassed within that dismissive phrase, "an indiscriminative mass society"? You almost seem there to be falling into a position as deterministic about literary invention as the one you believe "Mr. Roth" promulgates about human possibility. You describe the book as "farce with a thesis": yet, when you summarize in a few sentences the philosophical and social theses of the novel ("Mr. Roth's [book] blames society for the fate we suffer as human individuals and, legitimately or not, invokes Freud on the side of his own grimly deterministic view of life . . ."), not only is much of the book's material pushed over the edge of a cliff to arrive at this conclusion, but there is no indication that the reader's experience of a farce (if that is what you think it is) might work against the grain of the dreary meaning you assign the book—no indication that the farce might itself be the thesis, if not what you call the "pedagogic point." . . . May I suggest that perhaps "Mr. Roth's" view of life is more hidden from certain readers in his wide audience than they imagine, more imbedded in parody, burlesque, slapstick, ridicule, insult, invective, lampoon, wisecrack, in nonsense, in levity, in *play*—in, that is, the methods and devices of Comedy, than their own view of life may enable them to realize.[7]

The tone is not Roth at his best. He is telling, not showing—he knew he had to stop. Roth suddenly had so much to answer for, and answer he did, until the task simply became too tedious. It was then that he began his yearly escapes to Prague.

Arguably, Roth was responsible for depicting Jewish men as sexual predators, opening the floodgates of anti-Semitic attack. Or else he had depicted Jewish men as the sexualized victims of predatory Jewish mothers, incapacitated by guilt—stuck in marriages to nice Jewish girls and rendered incapable of social responsibility. One way or another, depending on whom you listened to, Roth had seriously spoiled things for American Jews. Either the anti-Semites have their field day, or our "whole modern human condition" loses its anchors. Shikse head, they win, Jewish tail, we lose.

Then, in December 1972—three years after publication, and quite out of nowhere—the unkindest cut of all. Irving Howe, who had had no small role in promoting *Goodbye*,

Columbus, published "Philip Roth Reconsidered" in *Commentary.* Howe, like Kazin, had himself rejected the debasing synagogue life of American Jews. If anyone was open-spirited (a favorite Howe phrase), bold, and subtle enough to recognize what *Portnoy's Complaint* was up to, was it not he? Nor would Howe, his integrity unimpeachable, write anything he had not thought about for some time. It was as if a rabbinic court of the New York Jewish intellectuals had decided on a *herem,* and Howe, erstwhile defender of the heretic, was enlisted to deliver the writ.

Portnoy's Complaint, Howe began, was neither anti-Semitic nor indecent. It was *worse,* a literary failure and a social disappointment. Picking up from where Trilling left off, but pressing the point with an authority about Jews and radical politics that she lacked, he revisited even Roth's early stories and wondered about the trajectory of his talent, his taste, and his future as a writer of fiction. *Portnoy's Complaint,* Howe feared, was proof that Roth would not live up to his potential. The book was useful only as a kind of social document: the ultimate expression of an immigrant "tradition" gone to seed in an America yet incapable of producing a fertile hybrid.

> Reviewers, including myself, . . . assume[d] that this
> gifted new writer was working in the tradition of
> Jewish self-criticism and satire—a substantial tra-

dition extending in Yiddish from Mendele to Isaac
Bashevis Singer and in English from Abraham Cahan
to Malamud and Bellow. . . . But now, from the
vantage point of additional years, I think it clear that
Roth, despite his concentration on Jewish settings and
his acerbity of tone, has not really been involved in
this tradition. For he is one of the first American-
Jewish writers who finds that it yields him no sustenance, no norms or values from which to launch his
attacks on middle-class complacence.

This deficiency, if deficiency it be, need not be a
fatal one for a Jewish writer, provided he can find
sustenance elsewhere, in other cultures, other traditions. But I do not see that Roth has—his relation
to the mainstream of American culture, in its great
sweep of democratic idealism and romanticism, is
decidedly meager. . . . [B]y now, simply to launch
attacks on middle-class suburbia is to put oneself at
the head of the suburban parade, just as to mock the
uprightness of immigrant Jews is to become the
darling of their "liberated" suburban children.

The problem, you see, was that Roth cozied up to a
tradition of Jewish writers while distancing himself from
its inspirations. But did he then embrace the realism of the
American tradition, its "democratic idealism and roman-

ticism"? He did not. This refusal might have been an opening for Howe to wonder if something new actually *was* going on, especially given the psychoanalytic cast of Roth's narrative. Might there be some as-yet unexplored tragedy lurking beneath the surface of "democratic idealism and romanticism" itself—not only the political economic hypocrisies which radical writers around *Dissent* ferreted out, or the moral hazards of Gatsby and the rest, but tragedy in a psychoanalytic cast, say, neurosis in the very promise of autonomy?

Howe was not impressed. Roth might have *believed* he was doing something new with *Portnoy's Complaint*, but all he was really doing was carrying on with an exhausted avant-garde or merely adolescent disgust of ordinary people: "Perhaps as a leftover from the culture of modernism and perhaps as a consequence of personal temperament," Howe continued, "Roth's two novels [before *Portnoy's Complaint*] betray a swelling nausea before the ordinariness of human existence, its seepage of spirit and rotting of flesh. . . . It is as if, in nagging at his characters, Roth were venting some deep and unmanageable frustration with our common fate." Nor was *Portnoy's Complaint* successful as a "modernist" text, since modernism— so Howe insisted—was passé, an expression of the shock of confronting middlebrow culture, or the shock of being belted-in to middle-class restraints.

Roth's (alleged) impatience with things "middle" bored Howe by now. *Portnoy's Complaint* was simply not going to impress him as a satire of manners, especially not Jewish manners. Portnoy attributes his sexual troubles to the guilt-soaked Jewish tradition, Howe writes. "But if we are to accept this simplistic determinism, why does it never occur to him, our Assistant Commissioner of Human Opportunity who once supped with John Lindsay in the flesh, that by the same token the intelligence on which he preens himself must also be attributed to the tradition he finds so repugnant—so that his yowl of revulsion against 'my people,' that they should 'stick your suffering heritage up your suffering ass,' becomes, let us say, a little ungenerous, even a little dopey . . . ?"

But wait, you might respond, this was Portnoy speaking, not Roth. Howe dismissed this answer, too. It was, he said, the weak line of defense against Roth's many critics that "Roth's admirers frequently man." Growing ever more adamant, Howe came to his main point. If Roth meant Portnoy to be an object of satire, then how good was the whole satiric show Roth was staging? Surely, Howe wrote, satire required Roth to hew closely to realistic detail, obliged "social accuracy":

He never shuts up, this darling Alex, nor does Roth
detach himself sufficiently to gain some ironic

distance. The psychic afflictions of his character Roth would surely want to pass up, but who can doubt that Portnoy's cry from the heart—enough of Jewish guilt, enough of the burdens of history, enough of inhibition and repression, it is time to "let go" and soar to the horizons of pleasure—speaks in some sense for Roth? . . . Portnoy is simply crying out to be left alone, to be released from the claims of distinctiveness and the burdens of the past, so that, out of his own nothingness, he may create himself as a "human being." Who, born a Jew in the 20th century, has been so lofty in spirit never to have shared this fantasy? But who, born a Jew in the 20th century, has been so foolish in mind as to dally with it for more than a moment?

Not surprisingly, Howe's attack made Roth sore. For Howe's phrase "obligation to social accuracy" was, when you think about it, the tradition of "democratic idealism and romanticism" at its most idealistic and romantic. No one could disagree with Howe's principle, that satire required "ironic distance" from what is complex, elaborated, experienced. And, yes, the word "Jewish" carried all the nuances of forlorn hope. Still, might a satirist not push the locus of reality into places Howe, for one, might be unwilling to go? And weren't Newark's suburban Jewish children as real—and imagined—as children in Tuneyadevske or, indeed, Winesburg, Ohio? What if Portnoy's patchwork of grievances, about his relations and himself, is about as close to real as a man *like him* can get? Portnoy, too, thinks that he *should* feel a certain comfort, gratitude, *nachas* (what David Kepish, the hero of Roth's later book *The Professor of Desire*, feels, for a few pages, anyway, true love and stable joy: "No more 'more,' and no more nothing either!")[8]

Roth might have expected Howe, of all people, to see that he had depicted the Jewish family as heroically nurturing in its way. There could be no humor if the love wasn't convincing. And there is from the novel's start the squishy love of the little boy for his mother—the sustaining conviction that his having been favored prefigured his worldly success ("Of me, the heir to her long Egyptian nose and clever babbling mouth, of me my mother would say, with characteristic restraint: 'This *bonditt*? He doesn't even have to open a book—'A' in everything. Albert Einstein the second!'"). There is, equally, abiding respect for a father's determination to keep food on the table ("'Alex,' he used to explain to me, 'a man has got to have an umbrella for a rainy day. You don't leave a wife and child out in the rain without an umbrella!'"). Portnoy was not up for making a Jewish family, but he had no doubts where real life existed. And our little Einstein was certainly smart enough, and reverent enough, to know that liberal America expected him to hold his own in more ways than one ("Why, in 1946, because they wouldn't let Marian Anderson sing in Convention Hall, I led my entire eighth grade class in refusing to participate in the annual patriotic-essay contest sponsored by the D.A.R."). What family, if not a Jewish family, had prepared him for the most bounteous years America had ever known? Could Howe not see that Portnoy was driving *himself* crazy with ingratitude?

I hasten to add that I knew and admired—no, loved—Irving Howe. I was among many young writers he nurtured up close. He needed no lectures from anyone, least of all from me, about the individuality of experience or the hubris of people who suppose social accuracy could be achieved through "positivism." As Howe writes in his own memoir, *A Margin of Hope*, "The best critics of all schools took for granted that a literary text merited respect for its integrity, but saw no reason to stop there. . . . Obeying the command of limit, they realized that it also signified there were stretches of perception beyond that limit, which one might yet bring to bear upon the literary work."

And yet, if I have to account for his decision to go after Roth, I can only assume that Howe's perceptions were being stretched beyond *their* limit by an implicit valorization of psychoanalytic tumult. Howe's first question to a sleepless friend (myself included) would be, "Are you making a living?" not, "Have you resolved your grief over your pathetic mother"? He approached disturbing novels (and his own insomnia, for that matter) with a worldly empathy and the odd Seconal. The really real was the factory, the office, the public square. Repression, too, was politically real, not a state of mind, or at least not a state of mind that had not first been shaped by larger political forces. Roth's book, in contrast, presumed to make a comedy of experiences that rivaled in their claim to being universal what lapsed Marxists looked for; primordial experiences like internal reckonings, including the incapacity to *enjoy* one's powers, even after society has endowed them in every reasonable way; experiences derived from buried quarters: what was pre-wired, what was familial, what was tragic in the tensions between parents and children.

Howe could not really buy the relevance of the psychoanalytic frame to primordial crisis. How then could he be expected to see Portnoy's complaints as necessary, or even excusable, literary constructions? It is "a weak line of defense" to see Portnoy as Roth's instrument if you cannot see (or just not sympathize with) what Portnoy might be instrumental to. For Howe, Portnoy's self-absorbed kind of freedom *distracted* from "social accuracy." Anyway, we were left with "dopey" complaints and Roth had inarguably written them.

Besides—Howe might have added (but didn't)—he had been there himself, in a crisis born of sexual desire, for much of the 1960s. He had concluded that with a little help from a worldly therapist one finally snaps out of it. (For the curious, Howe writes about this period affectingly in *A Margin of Hope*.) The point is, there was nothing about such crises epic enough to be worthy of extreme satiric treatment, not for Howe, not by 1972. Even if "darling Alex" were not a stand-in for Roth, how dare the author of *Portnoy's Complaint* imply that neurotic sexual kvetching was important enough to dwell on *this* much. People without historical vulnerabilities, natural enemies, et cetera, could afford to waste their time on such things, but Jews?

Besides, didn't Jewish sons especially owe their parents some respectful distance—fathers and mothers who had more or less run for their lives and then broken their backs to make their children safe? Given their children's American wings, and their own Yiddish weights, parents were bound to be heartbroken. How could this be funny? Why not soft-pedal the inevitable tensions? (Howe writes about his own father in *A Margin of Hope*: "In death he seemed terribly small, and I kept thinking back to all those years he had spent over the press iron, the weariness, the blisters, the fears, the subways. In the space that circumstances had grown up between us there still remained a glimmer of understanding, a tie of the sardonic.")

None of this means Howe disregarded what was personal or lacked tears. But for Howe, texts grew fascinating insofar as they had political context, political implication, practical bite: for him even the "desire to be a writer," so he mused in *A Margin of Hope*, always had to be reconciled "with remembered fantasies about public action." Self-absorption—even Emerson's self-reliance—tipped us into what was "bourgeois" in the saddest sense of the word. Immigrant Jewish parents somehow understood this: "Passionate about most things, the immigrants were shy about everything private," Howe goes on in *A Margin of Hope*, paying homage. "Many were intensely romantic, their escape from religious orthodoxy having been facilitated by sentiments adapted from European romanticism; but it was a romanticism shy of words, a reticent turning toward the idea of personality. And it was guarded by a decorum more rigid than shame."

Some will suspect that Howe's response to *Portnoy's Complaint* exhibited a generational jealousy of a different kind. He was the older man and the young Roth had become a kind of cultural star. An attitude of "let me encourage this young writer" might seem to have been replaced by "who does he think he is?" I reject this. Howe's problem with *Portnoy's Complaint* was what he said it was, that the book had become "a cultural document of some importance," and that what made it important was the same thing that made it symptomatic: "Younger Jews, weary or bored with all the talk about their heritage, have taken the book as a signal for 'letting go' of both their past and perhaps themselves, a guide to swinging in good conscience or better yet, without troubling about conscience." Moreover— here he echoed Scholem—Howe sincerely believed that American Jews could never really think themselves out of danger:

> For some Gentile readers the book seems to have played an even more important role. After the Second World War, as a consequence of certain unpleasant-nesses that occurred during the war, a wave of philo-Semitism swept through our culture. This wave lasted for all of two decades, in the course of which books by Jewish writers were often praised (in truth, over-praised) and a fuss made about Jewish intellectuals, critics, etc. Some literary people found this hard to bear, but they did. Once *Portnoy's Complaint* arrived, however, they could almost be heard breathing a sigh of relief. . . . [O]ne no longer had to listen to all that

talk about Jewish morality, Jewish endurance, Jewish wisdom, Jewish families . . .

Roth, just as sincerely, felt betrayed. Howe's attack wasn't exactly personal—though his allusion to Roth and his readers "swinging in good conscience" still seems something of a cheap shot. What rankled most with Roth was that Howe's own early essays on American Jewish families had once inspired him so. Who if not the radical Howe had seen through the synagogue, the pretensions of family propriety, the self-interested uses of liberalism? Who had had the courage to live like a scar on the map?

Perhaps the best articulation we have of Roth's frustration with (and affinity for) Howe was assigned to yet another character, Nathan Zuckerman, in *The Anatomy Lesson*. The critic "Milton Appel," so Zuckerman writes, had unleashed an attack on his career "that made Macduff's assault upon Macbeth look almost lackadaisical." Zuckerman muses:

> *He doesn't find me funny. Well, no sense writing to tell him to laugh. He thinks I depict Jewish lives for the sake of belittling them. He thinks I lower the tone to please the crowd. To him it's vulgar desecration. Horseplay as heresy. He thinks I'm "superior" and "nasty" and no more. Well, he's under no obligation to think otherwise. I never set myself up as Elie Wiesel . . .*

But long after the reasonable quarter hour had passed, he [Zuckerman] remained shocked and outraged and hurt. . . . One of Appel's own early . . . essays, written when he was just back from World War II, had been cherished reading among Zuckerman's friends at the University of Chicago. No one, as far as they knew, had ever written so unapologetically about the gulf between the coarse-grained Jewish fathers whose values had developed in an embattled American immigrant milieu and their bookish, nervous American sons. Appel pushed his subject beyond moralizing into deterministic drama. It could not be otherwise on either side—a conflict of integrities. . . . *Alienated, rootless, anguished, bewildered, brooding, tortured, powerless*—he [Appel] could have been describing the inner life of a convict on the Mississippi chain gang instead of the predicament of a son who worshipped books that his unschooled father was too ignorant to care about or understand.[9]

Curiously, Zuckerman thinks, Appel accuses him of self-pity and bitterness but his own generation of Jews was both better off and *less* bitter than Appel's. For Appel's father could speak to him easily only in Yiddish, and made his living from common labor. Both were a source of deep shame to the adolescent Appel. "Zuckerman, on the other hand, had a father who spoke in English and . . . [worked] in a downtown Newark office building . . . ; a father who'd read William Shirer's *Berlin Diary* . . ." Zuckerman's problem was that his father *half* understood. Indeed, Zuckerman's father had created a kind of halfway house, a place of American immanence and poise, which Appel's father had not. "Zuckerman wondered if there might not be more comedy in the conflict than Appel was willing to grant."

Yes, yes, this is Zuckerman and Appel, not Roth and Howe. Let's just say the "social accuracy" gets your attention. Nor would Roth have denied that, in spite of Portnoy's self-doubt and self-mockery, *Portnoy's Complaint* interrupted, in a way, a wave of philo-Semitism that had washed over America for a while. However, it had done so, not to express hostility toward Jews, but to register its doubts about philo-anything. Did not the morally superior pathos of Jewish intellectuals (much as Kingsley Amis rather too eagerly suggested) make Jews seem more condescending than attractive? Was not *Portnoy's Complaint* its own best evidence that American Jews were on to themselves? Portnoy again, obsessing about The Monkey, ironizing his inflated Jewish conscience:

But—what, what was I supposed to be but *her* Jewish savior? The Knight on the Big White Steed, the

fellow in the Shining Armor the little girls used to
dream would come to rescue them from the castles in
which they were always imagining themselves to be
imprisoned, well, as far as a certain school of *shikse*
is concerned (of whom The Monkey is a gorgeous
example), this knight turns out to be none other than
a brainy, balding, beaky Jew, with a strong social
conscience and black hair on his balls, who neither
drinks nor gambles nor keeps show girls on the side;
a man guaranteed to give them kiddies to rear and
Kafka to read—a regular domestic Messiah! Sure, he
may as a kind of tribute to his rebellious adolescence
say *shit* and *fuck* a lot around the house—in front of
the children even—but the indisputable and heart-
warming fact is that *he is always around the house.* No
bars, no brothels, no race tracks, no backgammon all
night long at the Racquet Club. . . . No, no indeed—
what we have before us, ladies and gentlemen, direct
from a long record-breaking engagement with his own
family, is a Jewish boy just dying in his every cell to be
Good, Responsible, & Dutiful to a family of his own.

Roth would put the matter rather more straightfor-
wardly in "Imagining Jews." The point was not merely
to deny the Jewish moral knight, but to deny it to its pur-
veyors at *Commentary* as well:

In brief: going wild in public is the last thing in the world that a Jew is expected to do—by himself, by his family, by his fellow Jews, and by the larger community of Christians whose tolerance for him is often tenuous to begin with, and whose code of respectability he flaunts or violates at his own psychological risk, and perhaps at the risk of his fellow Jews' physical and social well-being. Or so history and ingrained fears argue. He is not expected to make a spectacle of himself, either by shooting off his mouth, or by shooting off his semen, and certainly not by shooting off his mouth about shooting off his semen. That pretty much takes the cake. And in fact it did.

If it isn't obvious by now, I believe that Roth outlasted his Jewish critics for good reason; that *Portnoy's Complaint* didn't just take the cake, it finally allowed American Jews to have their cake and eat it, too. The cleverness, erudition, and liberalism of the confessions meant Jewish heroes played true to form. But by exposing a Jewish man in all his naked hunger and repressed aggression, Roth gave us the just the right stand-in for, of all people, an American Everyman. If a Jew is the last person you'd expect raw carnality from, and you can show just how badly a Jew wants, pursues, *demands*, then you pretty much have proof that you can expect this from the whole human race. (Item:

The Israeli journalist Danny Rubinstein told me that his childhood friend in Jerusalem imported pornographic films in the 1960s, and one of his biggest clients was—wait for it!—Gershom Scholem.)

"The scandal that accompanied this book, that it somehow denigrated Jewish life, was a mystery to me," James Carroll told me. "For me it was all about human liberation. But it was so far beyond anything that was possible in the Catholic world since Joyce. You would have had to compare it to the work of, say, Walker Percy, who was publishing very repressed, passive, secret stories—stories where you had to know the code to see that they were about a kind of sex that was not of a piece with the sacrament of marriage." Young Jews around the Diaspora felt the opportunity even more keenly. "For a certain type of Jewish boy," my friend Carlo Strenger, a psychologist at Tel-Aviv University, told me, recalling his reading of *Portnoy's Complaint*, not in America, but in a Swiss yeshiva, "ferocious sexuality is a means of individuation. It is your way of making sure that something of you is left that is not being touched or formed or intruded on by your upbringing—which is not true, in a way, since your sexuality then becomes very much shaped by the fact that it has become a tool or energy for individuation. The book is ostensibly about sex but it isn't. It's about how you salvage a core that is truly yours."

But of course the book had its biggest stage in America. By making Portnoy so hilarious and wild, ironically, Roth was punching our Jewish-American ticket. Hitherto, so he writes in "Imagining Jews," America's most celebrated Jewish writers, Saul Bellow and Bernard Malamud, had conditioned readers "to associate the sympathetic Jewish hero with ethical Jewhood as it opposed sexual niggerhood, with victimization as opposed to vengeful aggression, with dignified survival rather than euphoric or gloating triumph, with sanity and renunciation as opposed to excessive desire . . . except the excessive desire to be good and to do good." But if the relentless pretension to be good was not going to incite anti-Semitism, what was? (It was certainly enough to incite Portnoy against his own mother.)

There were, in other words, those who misread the book in the sense that making Jews repellent seemed an anti-Semitic task. But the goal of the book was not to get you to hate Jews. The book was *absent* a political goal. By letting Jews appear repellent, something happened. This was not actually the first time an author tried to make what happened happen. Back in 1934, also employing psychoanalytic frames, another Roth, Henry, had explored the fate of a Jewish family tortured in a more conventional way. His sublime novel *Call It Sleep* had sought to construct the consciousness of a young benighted hero,

David, whose tyrant father was his foil and mother was his Jocasta—a hero whose social and sexual appetites were dangerously warped by invasion and rage. But there was little comedy in *Call It Sleep*—some childhood sexual play in the closet, that's all. And without the comedy, Henry Roth had not much registered on young Jews in the 1940s and '50s. In all my conversations with him, Philip Roth never mentioned Henry Roth as an inspiration. Indeed, it wasn't until Kazin helped relaunch and champion *Call It Sleep* in 1964 that this novel finally found a significant audience.

I said at the start that everybody remembers where they were when they read *Portnoy's Complaint*. I do. What happened happened to me, too. My mother, warm, unstable, emotionally stunted, had unexpectedly died three years before and I felt a kind of terrible deliverance in my grief. My father—long estranged from her, in his third failing marriage—had lost his fortune and was losing his grip. (He would commit suicide a year later.) I know this all seems dreadful, and was, but I also knew a great deal of what was steady and interesting. I had an older brother and sister, skeptical of my big ideas, but loyal in our orphan-in-the-storm sort of way. I had teachers. I had descended into books. I was in my twenty-first year and already, a senior at McGill, married to my high-school sweetheart, Susan (now the celebrated Toronto-based artist Susan Avishai), both of us eager to put parents behind us and get on with things. I won't say more about any of this here, except that, through the chaos, and from the start, Susan and I felt our marriage vaguely "arranged," though it was we who had done the arranging. We had been afraid to upset families, guilty and square about our nakedness with one another, wondering if babies might redeem our baby-talk, or at least put what seemed missed-out-on into eclipse. I picked up *Portnoy's Complaint* expecting a laugh. I got a jolt. Its sexual frankness and hungers, its pleadings for autonomy, its *smartness*, brought what was in the back of my mind to the tip of my tongue.

And I was for purposes of this discussion a good Jew. Very good. I was impressively, deliberately, mature, sardonic, stoic: the president of McGill's big Hillel Society, a not-quite-observant but "respectful" son of a Conservative synagogue, a scion of a warm Zionist family from Bialystok. I had been the graduate of Hebrew summer camp, a former volunteer in Israel, picking pears and milking cows just after the Six Day War. My real liturgy was Pete Seeger's songbook—but I ate kosher-style. I knew what a *schande* was. Kafka, in that famous letter to his father, wrote that he sometimes imagined life as a map, and that his father's body was sprawled all over it, so that there was hardly any space for himself. My life as a man had begun before I knew what hit me, and yet personal difficulties paled next to the collective ones. Whatever the experiences of my home, we were "the spoiled brats of Jewish history," as Leon Wieseltier once put it. Desires, transgressions—all seemed folded into a feature of the Jewish Problem.

Then along came teenage Portnoy, telling Jews to stick their suffering heritage up their suffering ass, that he was also a "human being." I thought: a schande. I also thought, God, I need to grow up: be a little older and a little cooler, become the hero of my own story. My poor mother actually *had* said, often, that her problem was that she was "too good," by which she meant (but could not just say) too vulnerable, which really meant afraid of men. My father really did begin almost every conversation with the declaration that he was "worried" about me, about the choice between idealism (mine) and elbows (the world's), by which he really meant afraid for himself. Here, in *Portnoy's Complaint*, were all too familiar descriptions of Jews, some indeed obnoxious, yet a comedy of alienation derived from intimacy. That seemed the terrible truth.

Roth, in short, showed us what we knew in our bones, that the banality of evil was less a part of our experience than the evil of banality. ("Tell me something, do you know Talmud, my educated son? . . . Tell me, now that you are all finished at fourteen being a Jew, do you know a single thing about the wonderful history and heritage of the saga of your people?") It dawned on me, and many of my Jewish friends, that perhaps the thing to be most ashamed of was worrying *this* much about what there was to be ashamed of. The word had gotten around that Jews *were* human beings. No less than I was, non-Jewish friends were nervous wrecks, trying to pass exams, appease parents, find jobs, manage desire. Nothing would irritate them more than Jewish friends implying we were guiltier than everybody else, hence, perversely, morally above average. *Portnoy's Complaint*'s aggression seemed to drain resentments that had pooled around the claims of our Anti-Defamation League. Sexual anger, more than moral righteousness, gave Jews a chance to speak for the culture. Roth's book seemed a proof-text that America was home. (*Bernie, have you heard? Finally, a Jewish country and western song: "The Second Time She Said 'Shalom' I Knew She Meant Goodbye."*)

Roth once told me that he now finds the end of the novel, Portnoy's trip to Israel, its weakest part, the least dense, the most conventionalized. And, indeed, this seems to me the part where characters become personified categories. The earlier sketches yield to a narrative arc; things unfold according to some idea of what they might say, or *ought to* say. (Roth had escaped to Yaddo with his advance to complete this part of *Portnoy's Complaint;* the burlesque surrendered to storytelling.)

And yet I've always believed that this last part of the book, while the least performable and amusing, is most revealing of the real cultural choices American Jews then faced. For Roth brings his hero to a not altogether hypothetical place where exile is said to be superseded by homecoming—a naive move I had experienced at first hand during the 1967 war. If Portnoy's sexual psyche were his only problem—and he was just crazed enough by now to believe it was—then Israel just might be the place he could hope to have it all, banish "alienation," and, as Koestler's Joseph put it in *Thieves in the Night*, find a place where we all could "quit being Jews and become Hebrews," that is, quit struggling and "slip into a ready-made form."

And for young American Jews like myself, Portnoy's answer to Naomi ("Mr. Portnoy," she said, raising her knapsack from the floor, "you are nothing but a self-hating Jew." "Ah, but Naomi, maybe that's the best kind.") was perhaps the only line from the novel that immediately prompted a political thought that would last a lifetime. Suddenly, Zionism seemed to have an unexpected and compelling rival in America. Roth was hardly trying to start a Diasporist movement, like the crazed doppelganger "Philip Roth" of *Operation Shylock*; but as DeKoven Ezrahi puts it, Roth was reestablishing the virtues of a shlemiel's sense of irony, humble skepticism, naive humanism—a distancing from the sacred—that had made space for individual Jewish life in the Diaspora, certainly since the Emancipation. Inadvertent or not, this was a shot across Zionism's bow, or at least what Zionism had become in post-1967 America. It insisted on American Jews being more authentic, their experiences more open-ended, than Zionists were used to seeing.

Once, an exploded conversation in Jerusalem brought the submerged tensions to the surface. In the winter of 1988, at the beginning of the first Intifada, I arranged a lunch at the Knesset between Roth, with whom I was traveling, and Ehud Olmert, then a Likud backbencher, with whom I had become chummy over years of covering Israeli politics. Roth began straightaway asking Olmert how, in view of the mounting violence, Israel could really hope to keep territories populated by so many Palestinians. Olmert responded, with a complaint of his own, that the Palestinian revolt resulted from the fact that American Jews were "not coming" to settle there: presumably, two million American Jews flooding the territories would have rendered the claims of Palestinians moot. Roth suggested that American Jews might have ambitions of their own. Olmert dismissed these as "inauthentic."

The lunch quickly degenerated into raised voices and

hurried departures. But—a curious twist—Olmert told me recently that this lunch stuck in his mind and changed his view of the prospects for Zionism in America. "If a good Jew *like Roth* felt this way," Olmert said, "then what could be expected of the others?" (I did not have the heart to ask him what he meant by "good.")

Was there a peculiarly Jewish version of the American dream, one to contrast with life in Israel? If *Portnoy's Complaint* had had its way, I think, we should have stopped asking that question. Roth writes in "Imagining Jews" that the book undermines the idea that Jews might be prototyped in settled ways. Things simply don't work out this way. They don't work out at all. People might have "very strongly held ideas as to what a Jew in fact is, or certainly ought to be," Roth continues. But everyone from Theodor Herzl to Leonid Brezhnev to the Union of Orthodox Hebrew Congregations would tell you something different, that's the way it must be, and that's why you need writers to take Jews one at a time.

> In an era which had seen the avid and, as it were, brilliant Americanization of millions of uprooted Jewish immigrants and refugees, the annihilation as human trash of millions of Europeanized Jews, and the establishment and survival in the ancient holy

land of a spirited, defiant modern Jewish state, it can
safely be said that imagining what Jews are and ought
to be has been anything but a marginal activity of a few
American-Jewish novelists. . . . As I see it, the task for
the Jewish novelist has not been to go forth to forge
in the smithy of his soul the *un*created conscience of
his race, but to find inspiration in a conscience that
has been created and undone a hundred times over
in this century alone. . . . If he can, with conviction,
assent to that appellation and imagine himself to be
such a thing at all.

Needless to say, Roth's appeal remains at odds with
both neoconservative vigilance and the deterrent form of
Zionism that neocons celebrate. And if polls matter, it
seems American Jews share his skepticism even if this is
not reflected in headlines about American Jewish leaders
and the "pro-Israel" ideas reflexively attributed to Jews
as a whole. Some 70 percent of American Jews support
America's working to resolve the Arab–Israeli conflict and
exerting pressure on both Palestinians *and* Israelis. "Israel," as an "issue," ranks seventh (behind the economy,
health care, and so forth) in deciding Jewish voting behavior. About 60 percent of those under thirty-five feel
an attachment to Israel, but an even greater proportion
have never visited. They think of themselves as American

liberals; about half marry non-Jews.[10] Presumably, Portnoy's corresponding and self-satirizing humility suggests
weakness and invites attack; presumably, the very determination of American liberals to produce, or just presuppose, "a human race" suggests (as Ruth Wisse, the schlemiel's elegist, writes of Roth in a contemporary context)
unwillingness "to sustain a war against the anti-Semites
and the America-haters of our own time."[11] *Goodbye, Columbus*, hello Kishinev. But, really, what is more feckless
than the failure to grasp one's own powers, even the need
at times to protect others from oneself? Governments,
Madison taught, are not for Angels. What if not the di-
gestion of human shmutz has given Israelis the poise to
fight?

Okay, this is not the place to pick a fight, especially not
one Roth more or less won a generation ago. But it is
a fight that is never permanently won. The Jewish right
—though no more than 25 percent of American Jews—
shades into varieties of orthodoxy and express the political
culture Cousin Heshie was helpless against, one rooted in
nearly homogeneous Jewish neighborhoods and schools.
In recent times, neocons have claimed the public face
of American Jews, which has grown more proto-Zionist,
hard-line—indeed, more marginal to the vast majority of
Jews. So it is worth remembering that it was Alex Port-

noy, not Norman Podhoretz, who convinced America that its Jews had arrived. Ironically, Alex did so with recognizable human tragedy, much like Don Corleone, not Jimmy Durante—the *Godfather* was also published in 1969—persuaded Americans that Italians had arrived.

Were anti-Semites listening in on Portnoy's monologues, the whines, the rough talk of shikses and shvartzes? No doubt. Would this give them ammunition? Perhaps. But America in the 1960s was not some other place or other time. Asking about the ammunition that comes from satire was as queer as asking if the self-abasing *piyutim* of the Yom Kippur liturgy ("we sinned, we betrayed," et cetera) also gave anti-Semites ammunition. Anyway, who cared if it did, we dimly (and a little cockily) thought. Is it not the privilege of free citizens to care about their commonplace wounds?

Jews *did* have a body, even a body politic, as David Biale wrote in his ambitious *Eros and the Jews*. Portnoy's journey to the Promised Land showed how an eroticized Israel retained an enormous hold on the American Jewish imagination. But the journey also posed a counter-hero who, like most American Jews of the time, may have thought himself "incapable of achieving" what Israelis had, but was no less free in the enjoyment of aggression.[12] Moshe Dayan had made us ashamed of our fathers in ways Father Coughlin never could. But rumor had it that Roth and Moshe Dayan's writer-daughter, Yael, had had a thing for each other long before Portnoy and Naomi.

Christ, it was the self-subversive Portnoy who gave us the rhetorical platform to think out loud even about goyim—goyim as archetype to match our archetypal selves—and in frank ways that our future neocons never dared:

> Let the *goyim* sink *their* teeth into whatever lowly creature crawls and grunts across the face of the dirty earth, we will not contaminate our humanity thus. Let *them* (if you know who I mean) gorge themselves upon anything and everything that moves, no matter how odious and abject the animal, no matter how grotesque or *shmutzig* or dumb the creature in question happens to be. Let them eat eels and frogs and pigs and crabs and lobsters; let them eat vulture, let them eat ape-meat and skunk if they like—a diet of abominable creatures well befits a breed of mankind so hopelessly shallow and empty-headed as to drink, to divorce, and to fight with their fists. . . . Yes, it's all written down in history, what they have done, our illustrious neighbors who own the world and know absolutely nothing of human boundaries and limits.
>
> . . . For look at Alex himself, the subject of our

every syllable—age fifteen, he sucks one night on a lobster's claw and within the hour his cock is out and aimed at a *shikse* on a Public Service bus. And his superior Jewish brain might as well be *made* of *matzoh brei!*

In his 1967 memoir, *Making It,* Podhoretz claimed to have discovered the pleasures of "money, power, and fame." Compared with Portnoy's monologues, didn't this discovery seem a little fey? Jews with endless accusations against "anti-Semites and the America-haters" began to seem pathetic, incapable of self-reflection (or as Wieseltier would respond a few years later to Alan Dershowitz's sanctimonious book *Chutzpah,* "If you bleed us, are we not pricks?"). *Portnoy's Complaint's* Jewish readers were in this sense on much more intimate terms with America *and* Israel than the book's critics at *Commentary* suggested.

"Obviously, the problem for Alexander Portnoy," Roth writes in "Imagining Jews," "is that . . . nothing inflames his Jewish self-consciousness so much as setting forth on a wayward libidinous adventure—that is, nothing makes it seem quite so wayward than that a Jewish man like himself should be wanting the things he wants. The hidden Jew is unmasked in *him* by the sight of his own erection. He cannot suppress the one in the interests of the other, nor can he imagine them living happily ever after in peaceful coexistence."

A lustful Jew, a sexual defiler—an odd type in fiction, Roth suggests, because it is usually the goy who does the defiling in American Jewish fiction. It is *this* Jew, Roth's Jew, who brings the sigh of relief.

There is one last point to make here, already implied perhaps, but deserving separate treatment. Another of *Portnoy's Complaint*'s secular achievements, perhaps its most painful one, was to expose the cleavages in families living with the memories of immigrant sacrifices—families whose children did exactly what was expected of them, namely, get educated. The Portnoys were "second generation," the parents born in America. But the family as a whole was still living in the shadow of the old country. (Alex's Uncle Hymie, Heshie's tyrannical father, Alex's father's older brother, was born "on the other side" and still "talked with an accent.") The university was the best dream such parents had for their children. It also became their worst nightmare. For nothing undermined the prestige of loving parents like open-mindedness. Little by little, children drew away from their families, their frustration trumping their gratitude, their insistence on, say, rules of evidence undermining the very idea of tradition.

The showdowns might come over trivial things. Little

Alex refuses to put on nice clothes for the synagogue on
Rosh Hashanah. This turns the home into a seminary for
the kind of debate you imagine will only become more
freighted over the years:

"Look, I don't believe in God and I don't believe
in the Jewish religion—or in any religion. They're all
lies."

"Oh, they are, are they?"

"I'm not going to act like these holidays mean
anything when they don't! And that's all I'm saying!"

"Maybe they don't mean anything because you
don't know anything about them, Mr. Big Shot. What
do you know about the history of Rosh Hashanah?
One fact? Two facts maybe? What do you know about
the history of the Jewish people, that you have the
right to call their religion, that's been good enough
for people a lot smarter than you and a lot older than
you for two thousand years—that you can call all that
suffering and heartache a lie!"

"There is no such thing as God and there never
was, and I'm sorry, but in my vocabulary that's a lie."

"Then who created the world, Alex?" he asks
contemptuously. "It just happened, I suppose, according to you."

"Alex," says my sister, "all Daddy means is even if

you don't want to go with him, if you would just change your clothes—"

"But for what?" I scream. "For something that never existed? Why don't you tell me to go outside and change my clothes for some alley cat or some tree—*because at least they exist!*"

"You haven't answered me, Mr. Educated Wise Guy," my father says. "Who created the world and the people in it? Nobody?"

"Right! Nobody!"

"Oh, sure," says my father. "That's brilliant. I'm glad I didn't get to high school if that's how brilliant it makes you."

Such tiny cosmological exchanges may be sweet and rushed, but I'm not sure Christopher Hitchens ever really added to them. They are also terribly sad, portending a great drifting away. I remember how my own father once told me that life was "dog-eat-dog," and I responded, calmly at first, that Thomas Hobbes had said some such thing, but that he had been misinterpreted—that, actually, his war of all against all derived from the limitations of his epistemological assumptions (a point, in fact, I'll revisit in my Conclusion). I recall the excitement with which I used the word "epistemological" in this little debate, and then the odd sensation, that I might as well be driving a stiletto between his ribs. DeKoven Ezrahi observed that Roth developed the point about immigrants more completely, and without comic edge, in *The Human Stain*. There, the protagonist Coleman Silk is not an immigrant, exactly, but a light-skinned African-American prodigy, a generation away from the sharecropping South, who breaks irrevocably with his family to pass for a Jewish intellectual and thus enter the world of the university as an apparent equal. "*The Jazz Singer*'s motif is reversed," she says. "Instead of a Jew putting on blackface to make it in America, the black puts on a Jewish whiteface—but the trajectory is the same."

For Chinese-American writers like Amy Tan, the *Bildungsroman* builds much the same way: the travail of mothers and fathers setting the stage for heartbreak. Or think of the coming-of-age stories of South Asians in the film *Mississippi Masala*. For Israelis, there is another kind of assimilation, though it is the immigrants who determine the hegemonic culture and the native intelligentsia who "leave" for it. I once gave a Hebrew translation of *The Human Stain* to an Arab-Israeli friend, the novelist and journalist Sayed Kashua, who now writes exclusively in Hebrew. He stayed up all night to finish it. *Portnoy's Complaint* had had the same effect.

And it is in this sense precisely that the erudition of *Portnoy's Complaint* packs such a wallop. The deft language, the literary references, the social theories, the melding of *Logos* and *Eros*—all of these—suggest how the weapons Portnoy turns on himself are the very ones he had needed to realize his independence. The children of immigrants advance with a special burden, sickened by an inconstancy as sinful as infidelity. Oh, you *can* go home again, but with a kind of anthropological fascination that will seem a membrane between you and the people who, poor bastards, take your love for granted. Our wills become braided with skepticism, which boils down to demanding that the people around you must earn a right to an opinion. What chance do parents have?

Igor Webb, who reviewed *The Human Stain* in *Partisan Review*, said it all in a little digression:

> The jacket of my copy of Roth's second book, *Letting Go*, carries on the back a picture of him that, when I first saw it (in 1962!), produced in me a happy but also envious wave of emotion. A meticulously trim and neat—and ridiculously young—Roth is sitting in a rocker facing the camera. He has on a short-sleeve shirt open at the neck, chinos, and what used to be called, before the age of Nike, tennis shoes. On a low sidetable beside him is what seems to be a board game, the name of which you can make out to be Gettysburg.

So what's to be so emotional about? That the guy—this Jewish boy from Jersey—could be so palpably, photogenically American, so at ease in that New England-y rocker, so relaxed about claiming the culture (Gettysburg) for himself, so on top of goyishe informality, and yet—as the sneakers seemed to say in particular—so much, so simply, so autonomously, so *already* himself! That the guy seemed—to me, an immigrant survivor of the Holocaust with a new Americanised family name—to have beautifully, easefully overcome all the thorns and messes of having to pass.[13]

Roth, unsurprisingly, had taken to autonomy early on. As a child, he had attended Hebrew school in the afternoons. This did not heighten interest in Judaism. "Hebrew school wasn't school at all," says the hero of *Operation Shylock*, "but a part of the deal that our parents had cut with *their* parents, the sop to pacify the old generation—who wanted the grandchildren to be Jews the way that they were Jews, bound as they were to the old millennial ways."[14] There was not much exposure to old world Jewish culture in his home, but there weren't many books, or a phonograph, no music to speak of—not much of the best of American or Anglo-Saxon culture either.

Roth learned to read and write Hebrew well enough.

But he never much understood what he was reading or, curiously, developed an affinity for the Hebrew bible, even as a work of literature. He had a Bar Mitzvah, an event that stayed with him: the power on the podium, the insinuation of maturity. Mostly, there was the chance to make grandmothers happy. "It elevated the pathos of my relationship with my grandparents," he told me.

Jewish life meant, if anything distinct, a finely tuned fight against injustice. He had wanted to be a lawyer in high school, so it was no surprise that Roth made Portnoy a lawyer: "Politics came first from reading the novels of Howard Fast, who had had a column in the *Daily Worker*. But I had no strong attachments to unions or left social groups. For me it all came through FDR, whose picture was everywhere, in the barber shop, the shoe store. I was born the month he was elected. He was the Jews' president, the man for the underdog." One felt the Jews were horribly in danger around the world; in America there was residual discrimination and bigotry. "Otherwise, it was like being Swedish or Greek, different from the mainstream, but don't sweat it."

"If you forced me to admit that there is such a thing as a Jewish writer," Singer continued in that *Paris Review* interview, "I would say that he would have to be a man really immersed in Jewishness, who knows Hebrew, Yiddish, the Talmud, the Midrash, the Hasidic literature, the

Cabbala, and so forth." Roth transferred from Rutgers to Bucknell in 1951, and here "and so forth" stopped for him completely. He was drawn to the secular, intellectual side, one of those who—again, *Operation Shylock*—"had it in their heads to be Jews in a way no one had ever dared to be a Jew in our three-thousand-year history: thinking and speaking American English, *only* American English, with all the apostasy that was bound to beget." There was a Jewish fraternity, but he lasted in it only six months, mainly because he discovered books and found it hard to study with so much horsing around. The Jewish boys were studying finance and going into their fathers' businesses. He wanted to be closer to "whatever in Bucknell passed for Bohemia." He played Biff in a production of *Death of a Salesman.* (*What's the secret, Bernard?*) He loved American literature particularly, writers who took the stuff they knew about and made it "substantial."

Even in 1948, there had been no particular interest in his circles in the birth of Israel. Of course the global situation of Jews came through strongly, and the bigotry against Jews in America seemed as second nature as the muddled Jewish definitions that percolated in the home, synagogue, and playground. Roth heard from grandparents about immigrant life, that is, about the limitations grandparents presented. Yiddish seemed claustrophobic. It wasn't going to get you anywhere. English got you everywhere. Bucknell was a middle-class school, so there *had* to be kids from anti-Semitic households. Roth never ran into it. He had a Gentile girlfriend. More important, he had Gentile teachers, people who took to him and mentored him, day-in, day-out, neutralizing the Gentile phobia. "My closest professors never uttered the word Jew, or asked about this," Roth told me. "The enigma of the goy went poof."

The enigma of the goy went poof—in a way, a young American Jew's greatest relief. What remained, alas, was the enigma of the self. Which brings us to *Portnoy's Complaint*'s final, most subtle object of satire, the orthodoxies and templates of psychoanalysis itself.

CHAPTER FOUR

Punch Line

Psychoanalysis as the Object of Satire

By the end of the novel, Portnoy is dissolved in spiteful-ness. Naomi rejects him—so he tells Spielvogel, finishing up the story of his stay in Israel—and Portnoy lunges at her. This occasions his turning on himself and ultimately on Spielvogel, too:

> But what a battle she gave me, this big farm cunt!
> This ex-G.I.! This mother-substitute! Look, can that
> be so? Oh, please, it can't be as simplistic as that! Not
> *me!* Or with a case like mine, is it actually that you
> can't be simplistic *enough!* Because she wore red hair
> and freckles, this makes her, according to my one-
> track mind, my mother? Just because she and the
> lady of my past are off-spring of the same pale Polish

strain of Jews? This then is the culmination of the
Oedipal drama, Doctor? More farce, my friend! Too
much to swallow, I'm afraid! *Oedipus Rex* is a famous
tragedy, schmuck, not another joke! You're a sadist,
you're a quack and a lousy comedian!

Dr. Spielvogel, for his part, listens forbearingly. His
patient vindicates him before insulting him, manifesting
the self-pity no analyst could like and the one-track mind
some analysts love. Through it all Spielvogel maintains a
rock-like tranquility. Can we know who he is, this silent
Spielvogel, any better than Portnoy can?

Spielvogel makes only two appearances in *Portnoy's
Complaint* from which some kind of presence may be inferred. The first is as the referenced author of a professional article entitled "The Puzzled Penis" in *Internationale Zeitschrift für Psychoanalyse*. A putative abstract of the
article offers a definition of the disorder in question and
serves as the book's epigraph:

Portnoy's Complaint (pôrt′-noiz kəm-plānt′) *n*.
[after Alexander Portnoy (1933–)] A disorder in
which strongly-felt ethical and altruistic impulses
are perpetually warring with extreme sexual longings,
often of a perverse nature. Spielvogel says: 'Acts of
exhibitionism, voyeurism, fetishism, auto-eroticism
and oral coitus are plentiful; as a consequence of the

patient's "morality," however, neither fantasy nor act issues in genuine sexual gratification, but rather in overriding feelings of shame and the dread of retribution, particularly in the form of castration.' (Spielvogel, O. "The Puzzled Penis," *Internationale Zeitschrift für Psychoanalyse*, Vol. XXIV p. 909.) It is believed by Spielvogel that many of the symptoms can be traced to the bonds obtaining in the mother-child relationship.

The second appearance, in many ways prefigured by the first, is the last line of the novel, a deadpan if somewhat impatient response by Spielvogel to the primal yawp which issues from his patient after words, finally, fail:

PUNCH LINE

So [*said the doctor*]. Now vee may perhaps to begin. Yes?

Now, I have known serious people who consider Spielvogel's last words the saving grace of *Portnoy's Complaint.* They see the analyst as the novel's real hero whom Roth meant to valorize almost to spite himself. Or they see Spielvogel as a kind of proof that Roth has set up Portnoy as his *only* foil; proof that everything Portnoy says is to be taken as nothing but the issue from a tortured man-child, the swipes at parents, shikses, Israelis, et cetera, all just grist for the mill. "The book," writes the critic Maurice Charney in his 1981 study, *Sexual Fiction*, "is only the worthless ravings of a neurotic patient, who must dispose of all his garbage before the serious business of psychotherapy can begin. It is the wildness of *Portnoy's Complaint* that has endeared this book to so many readers, who participate in the frenzied and compulsive barrage of sex and aggression. The book offers release for our own bottled guilts about dirty words, masturbation, racial prejudices and other censored materials of the fantasy life."

Charney's reading was obviously meant to redeem Roth's reputation, which had been sullied, Charney implied, by uncharacteristically thick-headed Jewish critics who had missed the novel's nuance. Some practicing psychoanalysts I know, especially psychoanalysts of the old school, have been particularly sweet on Spielvogel. One eminent University of Chicago social scientist and psychoanalyst, when he found out I was writing about the novel, emailed me: ". . . one of my all time favorite books of intense and side splitting humor—because I grew up like that—my favorite line is the end—so now we SHALL BEGIN. Once you get out all the complaining about what everyone else did to you, it is time to start analysis and deal with your responsibility!"

Obviously, psychoanalytic practitioners do not mind that, in a book of great lines, the *punch* line belongs to the mysterious, venerable doctor—German syntax, knowing stillness, perfect timing—the hovering intelligence who, having waited with a Jedi's patience for you to finish your pleadings, tells you, with only a hint of condescension, to grow up. Some analysts admired Spielvogel's "intervention" so much they apparently concluded that, although Portnoy's complaints might be fictional, the doctor's answer to him was not. Indeed, one of the oddest responses to *Portnoy's Complaint* came from probably the most famous German-accented analyst in the world at that time, Bruno Bettelheim. He liked Spielvogel's stance so much, was so appalled by the patient's talk, and so identified with attacks by Jewish critics, that he seemed to forget that Roth invented Spielvogel, too. Writing in the Zionist journal *Midstream* (where Marie Syrkin was an editorial advisor), Bettelheim tried his own hand at satire, imagining what Spielvogel's "therapy notes" might look like, and thus presumably answering Roth in a language the little twerp could understand:

He is fascinated by his father's constipation, which is so stark a contrast with his excessive masturbation and incessant, diarrhea-like talk. It seems like an interesting fixation at the phallic level, where the father's constipation made him so anxious about the ability to produce that to compensate, he produces without interruption—whether by masturbating, talking, or intellectual achievement. If he does not learn to hold in, to store, but continues the indiscriminate discharge, analysis will certainly fail.

And, as if the patient were not sufficiently condescended to, Bettelheim's Spielvogel continues:

Clearly his promiscuity is one big effort to keep from his parents what they so much want, while making certain he is punished for it by getting nothing that is meaningful to him. For all his reading of psychoanalysis, he does not see that his promiscuity, particularly with gentiles, is one big reassurance that he is not having incestuous relations with his mother. By keeping his women ever-changing and meaningless to him, he remains faithful to his mother—not because she won't let him go but because he won't let go of her. Having enslaved himself to her, he projects the relation to see it as if she, or both parents, had enslaved him to them. . . . All he wants of me is to rid him of all the pangs of conscience he still feels about his selfish and asocial behavior.

Now, taking "responsibility" is a good thing (usually). One goal of psychoanalysis is to help us feel some gratitude for our powers, or for the improbable fact that we inhabit the planet to exercise them at all, not remain aggrieved by our failures (or the parents' failure to equip us for success)— as my analyst friend put it, "to deal." And Portnoy does come off addicted to his own pathos, especially in range of Spielvogel's authority, much like a child accustomed to crying his way to Reassurance—as if being hopeless can induce cosmic attention, while being responsible means being reconciled to the ordinariness of things, including the ordinariness of oneself (not the little "bonditt" who can get A's without opening a book, or the "big boy" whose rapturous coming gives women what no woman has ever got).

But, still, is Spielvogel a hero for our time any more than his patient is? I think not. Moreover, we are *meant* to think not. Both of Roth's attributions to him in *Portnoy's Complaint* signal that Spielvogel is fair game, too—that Roth's many-layered satire is of psychoanalytic orthodoxy, too. Indeed, with Spielvogel, Roth turns *Portnoy's Complaint* from a great farce into an unnerving mystery.

Start with the weakest signals, slipped in under the radar. I mean the epigraph and that parenthetical phrase "[*said the doctor*]," itself preceded by the curious title "PUNCH LINE." Forgive the pedantry, but we have no notion whose editorial decisions, words, or labels these are: Portnoy's retrospectively, or Portnoy *qua* author, a suddenly intrusive "narrator," or just Roth's? Okay, the mystery is not all *that* vexing. Your eyes pick up the cues and move on. But according to Spielvogel's special fans, the punch line was supposed to be the moment of climax. There was supposed to be an analysand and an analyst and an eavesdropping us. Suddenly, there is a meta presence in the text that supersedes the presence of the analyst. Spielvogel is subtly *denied* the last word.

Then there is the delicious title of Spielvogel's article, "The Puzzled Penis." It conjures a cartoon in the mind, yet it is close enough to *not* funny to leave one thinking that the analyst is being mocked for being half-serious. The idea that a man's penis thinks for him—and can even become ambivalent by thinking too much—just *might* be a psychoanalytic shorthand for male neurosis, a witty reversal of the famous Yiddish aphorism that Spielvogel could have been expected to know (indeed, the one Portnoy quotes against himself in the session: *Ven der putz shteht, ligt der sechel in drerd,* which Portnoy translates as, "When the penis stands, the brains get buried in the ground"). You can *almost* imagine an analyst of a certain dapper type regaling Upper East Side dinner parties with half-veiled stories of hard cases, preparing a sober article entitled "The Puzzled Penis." You can imagine him being so certain of his readers' gravity, of their pragmatic frankness, of their disproportionately "ethnic" origins, of their sense of control over prurient emotions, of their tendency to swamp scatological language with clinical theory and quantitative reasoning ("Acts of exhibitionism, voyeurism, fetishism, auto-eroticism and oral coitus are plentiful"), that Spielvogel would feel in no danger of undermining his science with a sly little joke.

Actually, the name of the journal in which Spielvogel publishes is itself a kind of joke. The *Internationale Zeitschrift für Psychoanalyse* was not just some portentous German name calculated to be comprehensible to a non-German speaker. The *Internationale Zeitschrift für Psychoanalyse* was *the* official organ of the psychoanalytic movement back when it was a movement. Roth's invoking of the journal's name implies how psychoanalysts were, from the first, themselves plagued by factionalism, excesses, and hubris of their own. According to the scholar Lydia Marinelli, research director of the Sigmund Freud Foundation, *Internationale Zeitschrift für Psychoanalyse* was an effort "to define strict limits in relation to other psychoanalytic schools emerging at the time," to "provide structures for scientific communication, even outside of congresses, between the different associations interested in receiving international psychoanalytic training"—in a word, orthodoxy.[1]

The journal was founded in 1913 by Sigmund Freud himself, with an editorial committee made up of Sándor Ferenczi, Otto Rank, and Ernest Jones. The first journal of psychoanalysis was closed down after a vote of "no-confidence" in the editor, Wilhelm Stekel, in November 1912. After World War I, following his dispute with Freud, Rank lost the editorship; in 1925 Max Eitingon, Sándor Radó, and Sándor Ferenczi replaced him. (After the Nazi rise to power in Austria in March 1938, the *Internationale Zeitschrift für Psychoanalyse* met its tragic end.)

The point is, when Spielvogel uses the word "perverse" in his abstract there is more than a vague idea of non-conformity behind it. He is faithfully mirroring Freud's own shrewd musings. "In the study of perversions," Freud writes in *Three Contributions to the Theory of Sex*, "we have gained an insight into the fact that the sexual instinct has to struggle against certain psychic forces, resistances, among which shame and loathing are most prominent. We may presume that these forces are employed to restrict the instinct to the accepted normal limits . . ."

What is the syndrome Spielvogel wants to cure Portnoy of if not what any reader of Freud would expect any young man to suffer from—*if*, that is, a number of crucial roles in the classical family were flipped around? A healthy sexuality was supposed to emerge out of infancy's oceanic feeling. There was *supposed* to be the nurturing mother and the sexualized little boy; there was *supposed* to be the totemic father whose forceful appropriation of the mother's body-and-desire turned said boy into a bundle of repressed rages ultimately shaping—dare I say it?—identity. (This is the structure of Henry Roth's family in *Call It Sleep*.) From here, so the drama continues, the man finally emerges, his fear of his father's castrating power leading to identification with the father's power, his post-guilty exercise of autonomy sanctioning the hunt for "appropriate" sexual partners. The climax is supposed to be gratification.

What, then, if the mother was a titan and the father a pussy? What if there is castration anxiety, but in this topsy-turvy family, it comes as a fear of not Daddy's power but Mommy's? Imagine that the superego comes as a low-voltage father who cannot stop struggling with his bowels. Imagine an oceanic feeling that persists well beyond infancy, the son *preferred* over the father. And what if the entire community seems to collude with this inversion? The totem that's torn down is self-conscious, preening, Jewish decency. What if the boy feels sorry for the father and responsibility for the mother, whose intimacies and demands are endless?

The author of "The Puzzled Penis," you see, had to have a pretty strong notion of healthy-mindedness for his patient's perversion to be systemic symptom. Portnoy's teenage masturbation, insatiable hunger, intrigue with shikse exotica, dread of Jewish incest, skepticism about marriage, pleasure in oral sex—all of these things—were telltale. In the back of his mind, Spielvogel had to be husbanding the concept of an immanently "responsible" Portnoy, *free* of perversions. "The ego must on the whole carry out the id's intentions," Freud writes in the "Dissection of the Psychical Personality" in 1932, "[b]ut only too often there arises between the ego and the id the not-precisely-ideal situation of the rider being obliged to guide the horse along the path by which it itself wants to go."

What if the rider, for anomalous reasons, is *afraid* of paths leading to primordial desire? Is it not enough to puzzle any penis? Push the thought experiment a little and you can almost feel Spielvogel's wish to spring his patient from neurotic pain to mere misery; to coach, worthily, the well-intentioned Jewish lawyer, warring with "altruistic impulses." With Spielvogel's help, the patient will dig a moat around his narcissistic desires, or at least domesticate them; he will relax into "genuine sexual gratification" after emancipating himself from his former naïveté, that is, mother-induced weakness and excessive empathy. In short, Portnoy, thanks to Spielvogel, will become a man in full: morally reciprocal, socially skilled, calm in crisis, comfortable in the missionary position.

If you read between the lines—and how can you not?—the über-objects of Roth's satire are these very orthodox psychoanalytic expectations, which Portnoy implicitly pays homage to by gushing out *this particular story*. I mean, it is so clear that our hero has read and internalized Freud as much as his analyst has—that he keeps imagining himself healthy in the classical way a well-analyzed man is expected to be, *wishing* he had a strong father, a guilt-free memory of mother, so that he could—according to the theory—stop pushing Naomis away or lusting for Monkey after Monkey. Portnoy, in other words, is relentlessly hoping for the very cure that the tut-tutting Spielvogel seems poised to supply. And Portnoy's self-dramatization has all the trappings of a transparent Freudian case, the making of an article that will almost write itself—full-throated *wanting* canceled out by self-destructive guilt. Would not this patient, alert to his analyst's expectations, be shrewd enough to construct precisely this drama—would not a patient whose presenting symptom is, among other things, a fear of his betters ("publicly pleasing my parents while privately pulling my putz!") not try privately pleasing his analyst?

Then there are the nights I will not eat. My sister, who is four years my senior, assures me that what I remember is fact: I would refuse to eat, and my mother would find herself unable to submit to such willfulness—and such idiocy. And unable to for my own good. She is only asking me to do something *for my own good*—and I still say *no?* Wouldn't she give me the food out of her own mouth, don't I know that by now? . . .

Which do I want to be when I grow up, weak or strong, a success or failure, a man or a mouse?

I just don't want to eat, I answer.

So my mother sits down in the chair beside me with the long bread knife in her hand. It is made of stainless steel, and has little sawlike teeth . . .

Doctor, *why*, why oh why oh why oh why does a mother pull a knife on her own son? I am six, seven years old, how do I know she really wouldn't use it? What am I supposed to do, try bluffing her out, at seven? I have no complicated sense of strategy, for Christ's sake—I probably don't even weigh sixty pounds yet! Someone waves a knife in my direction, I believe there is an intention lurking somewhere to draw my blood! . . . Suppose she had let me win— what would have been lost? Why a *knife*, why this threat of *murder*, why is such total and annihilating victory necessary—when only the day before she set down her iron on the ironing board and *applauded* as I stormed around the kitchen rehearsing my role as Christopher Columbus in the third grade production of *Land Ho!*

Why, indeed, a knife? Portnoy's fear and trembling leads inexorably to a Freudian altar.

Or take another scene. The eleven-year-old Alex Portnoy is shopping for a bathing suit with his mother, so the narrating Portnoy recalls: "'I want one with a jockstrap in it!' Yes, sir, this just breaks my mother up. 'For *your* little thing?' she asks, with an amused smile." What purveyor of psychoanalysis's standard template ever dreamt of applying it to a patient this quotable in *Internationale Zeitschrift für Psychoanalyse*? Could it be that Portnoy's analyst, something of an orthodox practitioner himself, had not been able to stop himself from suggesting to his patient, again and again, some overdetermined family drama proving the consistency of his own theory?

Roth was by no means the first to suggest that patients tell analysts what they want to hear. Freud writes in *Mourning and Melancholia* that very distressed patients will particularly abase themselves, that is, to preempt what they assume will be an impending analyst's criticism. "Shame before others," he writes, "is lacking . . . , or at least there is little sign of it; one could almost say that the opposite trait of insistent talking about himself and pleasure in the consequent exposure of himself predominates." The melancholic's behavior does not *seem* that of a person who is devoured by remorse and self-reproach. But he or she has lost self-respect—"and must have some good reason for having done so." Freud concludes: "It is the mental faculty commonly called conscience that we are thus recognizing. . . . [D]issatisfaction with the self on moral grounds is by far the most outstanding feature."

Portnoy's talent for self-effacement, one might say, conformed to this pattern; Roth was implicitly counting on readers to pick up the cues. Through the comedy, the self-mockery, is a patient's loss of dignity. Portnoy is overwhelmed by "conscience," ambivalent about his own judgment, holding himself together by showing off his psychological virtuosity, in this case, his genius for poking at himself in ways that are expected of him. His misfortune (and our entertainment) is that he thinks he has to present himself in a comic mode. Portnoy has not yet understood the purpose of the encounter, which is to transcend this impulse to see himself as heroic and, therefore, an object of his own brave derision. Portnoy's stories are full of charming revelation and psychoanalytic play—also fierce anger at family and tribe—but they are almost entirely at his own expense. Portnoy seems always to be beating Spielvogel to the punch.

He recalls his soiled underwear: "I deliver forth—deliberately, Herr Doctor, or just inevitably?—the fetid little drawers of a boy." That third dimension (*deliberately, Herr Doctor, or just inevitably?*) is what leaves readers on edge, unsettled, the way you feel after the class clown finishes his antics and you aren't sure if you have been laughing with him or at him and you sense *he* isn't sure either. Or think again of Portnoy's venture to Israel. You might expect Portnoy to want fellow-feeling from Spielvogel, of all times, here. But he relates the scenes of his rage and impotence as if some scold were poised to strike. ("Let's see somebody beat that, for acting out! Could not maintain an erection in the Promised Land! At least not when I needed it, not when I wanted it, not when there was something more desirable than my hand to stick it into . . .")

Portnoy's stories, in other words, seem there to explain why skepticism *would* be the stance of any listener. In the face of Spielvogel's authority—which the analyst may pooh-pooh as transference, but which cannot be *entirely* transference, since the analyst calls the patient "patient" and accepts hundreds of dollars a week—Portnoy's suffering must seem to himself no worse than what he deserves. By the end, Portnoy is treating his insecurities almost entirely with this combination of self-sarcasm and bravado. You find yourself reading, impressed, entertained, *identifying*, yet vaguely repulsed and apprehensive for him. You laugh out loud, but the facetiousness can wear out its welcome.

Roth shows, without quite showing his hand, that the

psychoanalytic vernacular can be just another material with which self-hatred works. Roth's novel reaches its anticlimax—the only climax the book really has—with Portnoy surrendering. So much admission of moral failure, so much grief and so much (if the patient could only see it!) *genuine* failure rooted in the neurotic *fear* of failure. He seems to be saying, "See how narcissistically and self-destructively I wished for freedom only to become a disappointment to myself; see, on the other hand, how willing I am to live on the tragic plane as penance for the emotional crime of *unhappiness*. Sure I will lie here and *try* to be happy. But catharsis is for sissies!"

And, in all of this, Spielvogel maintains his impartiality, his very reticence bringing Portnoy to tease out the moral arguments with which he reviles himself. His serenity implies to Portnoy a more spacious, more self-assured universe than the one Portnoy is now choking on. Spielvogel seems a moral test and the personification of how one qualifies to take tests. For alert American readers, this may be the biggest transference since the Louisiana Purchase. "Once you take the categories of illness and health seriously," Roth told me, "then you are leaving the atmosphere of this book—then you are beginning to impose *another* vocabulary—and a foreign and *alien* vocabulary—on this book." Indeed, of all the orthodoxies undermined in *Portnoy's Complaint*, psychoanalytic orthodoxy may be the most insidious because it is the most hidden.

Hans Kleinschmidt, the New York therapist with whom Roth was finishing analysis as he was starting up *Portnoy's Complaint*, specialized in treating creative artists. His patients included Richard Avedon and Leonard Bernstein. Kleinschmidt's office had, at first, been a refuge for Roth during the tortured negotiations to secure a divorce from his first wife (as fate would have it, she was killed in a car accident in the days before *Portnoy's Complaint* was published). By the end of the analysis, which had started in 1963, Kleinschmidt's specific interpretations of Roth's blues often seemed to his patient more useful as material than as a springboard to self-discovery.

In a way, *Portnoy's Complaint* was Roth's cunning tribute to Kleinschmidt's blinkered and dogmatic claims. The process of analysis had been helpful, a place for confidentiality, a way of keeping track. By the end, the insights and pains had been talked out. And yet the analysis was often misguided, which might have been predictable given Kleinschmidt's origins. He was a German Jew. He had been educated in Berlin; then he went to Italy when Hitler came around; he finished his medical school in Bologna. Then he made his way to America in his middle twenties. He was a gifted man, mostly interested in art.

He collected Kandinsky. He had many painters for patients. But, inevitably, he lacked context for American
Jewish families. He may well have imagined himself superior. "He knew nothing about us," Roth remembers, "but
he had this mythology." Curiously, it was much like those
Jewish student stories at the Iowa Writers' Workshop—
nebbish father, domineering mother:

"Kleinschmidt, inadvertently, *gave* me *Portnoy's Complaint*. The book was a not a simple satire, really, but a
playful rendering of the American Jewish family that came
out of this folklore. Kleinschmidt would say, 'Maggie,
does she remind you of your mother?,' and I would say,
'Not in the least.' Nobody who knew my mother, could
confuse her in any possible way with this character. She
was so *comme il faut*." It was the same thing with the father. "Kleinschmidt had the notion that my father was
weak. But I knew from being with my father that he wasn't
weak. He was a rock: indestructible. He was knocked down
and he got up again; he was solidity. I knew he had a lowly
position in the world, at a life insurance firm, though
even that changed after the war when he was promoted. I
knew where we stood compared to the wealthier parts of
the community. But my father represented tenacity, and
grit, and courage—I never doubted that for a second. It's
what gave me *my* tenacity.

"But he, Kleinschmidt, had it otherwise. It frustrated

me terribly, but he gave me a good idea. It was a *better*
family to use than my family. It was the poor father. The
weak Jewish father, overwhelmed by the mother. And
that's around the time I went to Iowa, to teach writing,
where I had a disproportionately high number of Jewish
students. And, again, they'd write about this folk family.
Their stories may have been true in their detail, but never
mind: the stories were *organized* around this folklore. I
said [as if to Kleinschmidt]: 'Okay, you want this Jewish
family? I'll *give* it to you!'"

The stereotype became a way to enact the theory. Here's
what Freud looks like—here's what Freud *smells* like, or
sounds like. You want an Oedipus complex? The family
will play out something worse than Oedipal tension. It will
play out Oedipal victory. (*Der mensch tracht und Gott lacht,*
my poor father used to say: Men strive and God laughs.)
Actually, Roth's real family inspired, or half inspired, the
character of Portnoy in only one way, which he and I
found ourselves talking about, unexpectedly, during the
sad aftermath of the death of Roth's older brother, Sandy,
a noted painter and advertising executive, who had suffered from crippling illnesses in his later years, and who
died in Chicago in the spring of 2009 at the age of eighty-
one. Roth told me on the phone after the funeral that
Sandy had now and then complained that recurrent feelings of ineffectuality might be attributed to their mother's

overweening watchfulness—something Roth himself did not feel, but which impressed him as a feature of Sandy's self-examination. For Roth's part, his mother's celebration of him had always seemed a part of what became artistic poise.

Roth remembers his analyst kindly, but the high comic moments in *Portnoy's Complaint* turn psychoanalytic authority against itself by taking its projections to extremes. Freud had made incessant lust natural. Portnoy says "I fucked my family's dinner!" as if it were a kind of coup. The confession is *structured* to be comical, to make him, and his "drives," ridiculous—to make the language suspect. Which brings us to another essay, in another professional journal:

"Traditional psychoanalytic thought," the author-analyst writes, "has it that narcissism as a dominant defense indicates a regressive phenomenon; but this point of view seems to overlook the aggressive aspects of such a defense." ("Regressive," in this case meaning childlike passive-aggression, I suppose, would be at odds with an adult's overt aggression.) The author continues: The creative person is thus *fundamentally* aggressive; he will be unforgiving of parents and, consequently, never let any woman get close.

The push to create, therefore, serves several ego functions: First of all to justify the feelings of uniqueness and the rage implicit in the rejection of the significant figures. The narcissistic defense poses an *ideal self* which finds fruition in the creative endeavor. The ideal self or the unique identity achieved through the creative act justifies the aggression toward the mother since if the artist is unique, his dissatisfaction in that relationship is warranted. The guilt over such aggression results in feelings of unworthiness which can only be offset by a further push toward narcissism.

Another function of the creative push is the search for the "perfect" communication of feeling; the quest for this perfection is the quest for total understanding and, thereby, acceptance and, hence, ideal love.

Then again, the pronounced narcissistic character helps to restore some semblance of balance within the ego, constantly threatened by the tremendous anger at parental figures, and, subsequently, all authority. A person with such enormous narcissism is always saying to himself: "How dare they?" The stance of never forgiving the parents and thus never really allowing anyone to get close is the primitive defense against the fear of ego disintegration.

More Bettelheim posing as Spielvogel? Spielvogel, in a sequel to *Portnoy's Complaint*? Actually, the words are from an article entitled "The Angry Act: The Role of Aggression in Creativity," published by Hans J. Kleinschmidt, in the Summer/Spring 1967 issue of *American Imago*—the then preeminent scholarly journal of psychoanalysis, which had been founded by Sigmund Freud and Hans Sachs in the tragic year of 1939, not long after the closing of *Internationale Zeitschrift für Psychoanalyse*.

In "The Angry Act," Dr. Kleinschmidt's case studies are mostly of famous artists whom the author encounters through biographical glosses: Kandinsky and Thomas Mann and Giacometti and Sylvia Plath ("Daddy I have had to kill you. / You died before I had time . . .") and John Keats. But about three-quarters into the article, the author reveals the case of a "Southern playwright in his early forties" who had presented himself for therapy because of "anxiety states experienced as a result of his tremendous ambivalence about leaving his wife, three years his senior." The playwright, it soon became clear, suffered "castration anxiety vis-à-vis a phallic mother figure." He was six when he threatened to leave home because of his displeasure with his mother's discipline. He remembers that, at one point, his mother packed a little bag for him, and told him to go ahead, "but then he suddenly found himself outside the locked door while trying in vain to get back inside by hammering at the door and crying to be permitted to come back." He may have been eight or nine years old when he still fantasized "that his teachers were really his mother in disguise who in some very clever magic way would get home quickly and be there by the time he returned from school."

Oh, the author of the "The Angry Act" had one more memory to share from his anonymous patient:

> He was eleven years old when he went with his mother to a store to buy a bathing suit. While trying on several of them, he voiced his desire for bathing trunks with the jockstrap. To his great embarrassment, his mother said in the presence of the saleslady: "You don't need one. You have such a little one that it makes no difference." He felt ashamed, angry, betrayed and utterly helpless.

His patient thus went off the rails. Because of his castrating mother, he was forever incapable of "normal" love, but was certainly suffering the ravages of creativity. "The writer felt at an early age that he was different from his parents. His father was ineffectual and submissive to the mother. He was aware from the age of nine that he perceived events with more sensitivity than his family or his peers." But since a mother-child relationship "was definitely established," the writer was "able to use narcissism as a defense against anxiety" engendered by the prospect of separation from her.

It is not hard to imagine what the Northern novelist in his late thirties would feel reading about this Southern playwright in his early forties, in an (albeit, obscure) article published just around the time the corresponding comic parts of *Portnoy's Complaint* were becoming ubiquitous in various literary magazines. It is not hard to imagine the feelings of betrayal—not hard at all, in fact, because Roth would soon work up the episode fictionally in his 1974 novel, *My Life as a Man*, about which more presently. This is not to say Roth knew about Kleinschmidt's article when he wrote *Portnoy's Complaint;* I am not suggesting the novel is some kind of answer to it. What the article reinforces is Roth's impression of the kind of conversation Kleinschmidt conducted with him—the family saga he *needed* to assume in order for his theory of narcissistic aggression in creative people to be validated.

For Roth to have captured this trope in his psychiatrist's "fiction," even while pained and embattled—even while appreciating Kleinschmidt's refuge and empathy— gives a whole new meaning to the term *tour de force*. Roth worked this material further, developing the fictional Spielvogel into a full-blown character in *My Life as a Man*. His fictional psychiatrist writes an article about creative artists—painters, poets, and novelists—including about his patient, the novel's protagonist, Peter Tarnopol. This article, too, assumed a patient whose central problem was—I quote from *My Life as a Man*—"castration anxiety vis-à-vis a phallic mother figure."

The implication that the fictional patient in *My Life as a Man* cannot help but draw from this diagnosis is that the failure of his marriage, indeed his willingness to marry in the first place, had been his own fictional fault. Tarnopol, devastated but brave, answers Spielvogel much like you'd expect Roth to have answered Kleinschmidt. That's not my mother; that's not my father; I got married at the tender age of twenty-six, for God's sake. I had been naive, unable to suss out ruthlessness, not subconsciously courting disaster (though, self-effacingly, a short story Tarnopol writes about his marriage is called "Courting Disaster"). And Tarnopol's most important questions regarding the article are not about Spielvogel's stubbornness regarding his family, but rather about the limitations of Spielvogel's *imaginative rendering* of writers' imaginations in general. The psychiatrist Richard M. Gottlieb took up the point, and Tarnopol's defense, in a little unpublished paper he shared with me about *My Life as a Man*, which he called "Tarnopol's Complaint": "To write about another person (as I am now writing about Roth) is to objectify that person, to do him violence, betray him, to distort his experience, and to shoehorn his identity into language that can never be so precise as to be accurate." (The problem, as Roth himself told me, is what people call "reductionism.")

Back in 1984, Roth had told Hermione Lee in the *Paris Review:* "If I hadn't been analyzed I wouldn't have written *Portnoy's Complaint* as I wrote it, or *My Life as a Man* as I wrote it, nor would *The Breast* resemble itself. Nor would I resemble myself." He continues:

> The experience of psychoanalysis was probably more useful to me as a writer than as a neurotic, although there may be a false distinction there. It's an experience that I shared with tens of thousands of baffled people, and anything that powerful in the private domain that joins a writer to his generation, to his class, to his moment, is tremendously important for him, providing that afterwards he can separate himself enough to examine the experience objectively, imaginatively, in the writing clinic. You have to be able to become your doctor's doctor. . . . [S]o many enlightened contemporaries had come to accept the view of themselves as patients, and the ideas of psychic disease, cure, and recovery. You're asking me about the relationship between art and life? It's like the relationship between the eight hundred or so hours

that it took to be psychoanalyzed, and the eight or so hours that it would take to read *Portnoy's Complaint* aloud. Life is long and art is shorter.

There is a measure of truth to the idea that writers, indeed all artists, act out of a raging self-doubt. What interview with Terry Gross on *Fresh Air* starts without a knock on that door? And we all know intimidated people who console themselves with idealized versions of themselves; people who may search for distinction as a "successful" artist because, discounted as children, they dream of a world in which their reputations will precede them like artillery. These same people may long, much as Kleinschmidt assumes, for some perfect communication with people in general, that is, to make up for the inability to talk with parents in particular. There may be aggression lurking behind literary ambition—okay, there *must* be.

But why assume guilt over, say, a fanaticized retaliation against a domineering mother is the most likely explanation for this fear? There are so many other ways people can feel small in a big universe. If there is aggression to the creative act, might this be nothing more, or less, than a kick against the forces that pull us back into the dust? The problem with Spielvogel, Tarnopol says, is that he is simply not an imaginative enough writer of fictions:

. . . And while we're at it, Dr. Spielvogel . . . you
cannot begin to make sense about "creativity" or "the
artist" or even "narcissism" if you're going to be so
insensitive to fundamental distinctions having to do
with age, accomplishment, background, and vocation.
And if I may, sir—his *self* is to many a novelist what
his own physiognomy is to a painter of portraits: the
closest subject at hand demanding scrutiny, a problem
for his art to solve—given the enormous obstacles to
truthfulness, *the* artistic problem. He is not simply
looking into the mirror because he is transfixed by
what he sees. Rather, the artist's success depends as
much as anything on his powers of detachment, on
*de*narcissizing himself. And that's where the excitement comes in. That hard *conscious* work that makes
it *art!* Freud, Dr. Spielvogel, studied his own dreams,
not because he was a narcissist, but because he was a
student of dreams. And whose were at once the least
and most accessible of dreams, if not his own?[2]

Spielvogel's limitations are almost always paradigmatic.
Rigidity asserts itself in spite of his avowed appreciation
for complexity. You cannot present your family to him and
not expect the Oedipus Complex any more than present a
political problem to Alan Greenspan and not expect Free
Enterprise:

Why don't you believe me? Why, to substantiate your "ideas," do you want to create this fiction about me and my family, when your gift obviously lies elsewhere. Let *me* make up stories—you make sense! . . . Did it ever occur to you, Doctor, in the course of your ruminations, that maybe *I* was the one who was made into a sexual object? You've got it all backwards, Spielvogel—inside out! And how can that be? How can you, who have done me so much good, have it all so wrong? Now *there* is something to write an article about! *That* is the subject for a symposium![3]

Spielvogel's fictional article does not reach any great number of people—no more than Kleinschmidt's *un*fictional one. But for Tarnopol, as for Roth, this was not the point. What was most infuriating was not one's analyst's exposure of memories that cupped into published stories, or even the experience of having him label one a narcissist in a professional journal while critics in popular magazines (and with a dim understanding of what narcissism means) were doing the same thing. No, most infuriating was the sheer arrogance of bad fiction:

> "Just read on" [Tarnopol tells his partner Susan about Spielvogel's article]. "Read the whole hollow pretentious meaningless thing, right down to the footnotes from Goethe and Baudelaire to prove the connection

between 'narcissism' and 'art'! So what else is new?
Oh, Jesus, what this man thinks of as *evidence!* 'As
Sophocles has written,'—and that constitutes *evidence!*
Oh, you ought to go through this thing, line by line,
and watch the ground shift beneath you! Between
every paragraph there's a hundred-foot drop!"[4]

To "do one's part for fiction," Roth told that interviewer, is pretty much all we have. To do it well, however,
you first have to acknowledge that you are doing it at all.

Portnoy's Complaint's implied satire of psychoanalytic reductionism may have been a rather elite way of affecting
some larger American culture, but it trickled down like
Goldman Sachs bonus money in lower Manhattan. After
Portnoy's Complaint and *My Life as a Man* were published—
not because of them, but *along* with them—acolytes of
Donald Winnicott, Alice Miller, Anthony Storr, Jacques
Lacan, Melanie Klein, and many others enjoyed something of a heyday. For many, the term "psychoanalysis"
came to connote more of an existentialist mourning than
a clinical curing; and as Janet Malcolm acknowledged in
her book *Psychoanalysis: The Impossible Profession* (1981),
many educated people turned on psychoanalysis of the
"unswerving classical Freudian sort" the way a Protestant
might turn on Papal Infallibility.[5] "Part of *Portnoy's Com-*

plaint is a parody on psychoanalytic technique, the kind of thing you assume about the way psychoanalysis was practiced in New York and the 1940s, '50s, and '60s," the Tel Aviv psychologist Carlo Strenger told me. "The caricature pivots on the neutrality a great many psychoanalysts tried to assume at the time, which may itself have been attributable to a simple fact: many of them were immigrants from German-speaking countries and felt completely out of their depth in American culture. Neutrality was probably more a kind of frightened holding back than anything else. Of course, we work very differently today. As someone who has done thousands of sessions I can tell you we're much more interactive, we don't see ourselves as objective mirrors, but rather as participant observers."

Roth was a part of the background to this change, his Zuckerman novels and the enigmatic legacy of *Portnoy's Complaint* pushing psychoanalytic talk away from "sickness" and "health," "normalcy" and "perversion," and toward insistence on the uncertain details of experience, a recognition of the tragic—in short, a kind of humility that becomes a real because permeable fortress against the assaults of the world. "Roth," Strenger added, "certainly had a big part in discrediting the classical psychoanalytic notion that if you can understand it, it will dissolve. Actually, we do not break out of what Kundera calls our basic 'existential equation.'"

This is not the place (and I am not the writer) to pursue the point very far. I do not mean to judge Hans Kleinschmidt, whom I never met except in print, and who is reputed to have helped a great many people. Nor do I presume to dismiss the virtues of psychoanalysis, of which I am a grateful beneficiary. I certainly do not wish to imply any satisfaction with the degree to which the practice of psychoanalysis has fallen victim to chemistry and skeptical accountants. Malcolm makes clear that the phenomenon of transference, "how we all invent each other according to early blueprints," remains Freud's most original and radical discovery. It suggests that personal relations are inevitably "a messy jangle of misapprehensions, at best an uneasy truce between powerful solitary fantasy systems"—that "we cannot see each other plain"—a characterization of our tragic connections that Roth, with qualifications, no doubt would accept. As Adam Gopnik, himself a former patient of Kleinschmidt, put it to me, "Nowadays, Portnoy would go to Spielvogel and the doctor would have to give him Prozac and Viagra and send him home."

And there is even something to be gained from the reductive ways Kleinschmidt's article put the case for narcissism (though Tarnopol feels the word is used against him "like a club").[6] It implies that creative people will need to have a reservoir of selfishness to carry on in the face of indifferent critics. Good writing shakes readers up and doesn't always bring praise or money. Even if the article's explanation for exceptional egoism is rooted in a shopworn paradigm, you can see how regular visits to an analyst armed with Kleinschmidt's theory could take a wounded writer through a difficult period. If you are quickened by doubts, it cannot hurt to have someone taking the side of your "ideal self."

Gopnik agrees. "Kleinschmidt never offered me any kind of classical Freudian account to organize my experience. I saw him in the 1990s, and his approach may well have been different in the 1960s. Instead, and that was part of the comedy of it, he was immensely practical and opinionated. He had a deep tropism towards Freud but he never seemed to make me explain what I was feeling in terms of Freudian theory. He had the beautiful irresponsibility of old age, and offered me counsel, advice, disapproval, anger and so forth. Kleinschmidt's central message to his patients"—so Gopnik continues—"was that you don't want to overcome your narcissism, or self-attention, but you want to use it to build an impregnable fortress that will defend you from the world; that the relationship between narcissism and creative anger is built-in, and anyone who is an artist, photographer, novelist, comedian, has to use it—but use it in a productive and self-defending way, rather than in a neurotic and vulnerable way."

Tarnopol, too, finds a kind of grace in Spielvogel, even after confronting his treachery. The doctor suggests that if trust has been undermined, then perhaps the analysis should be discontinued. This puts Tarnopol into a panic. No, no, he insists. The sessions must continue:

> Because I'm scared to be out there alone. Because things in my life *are* better. . . . What I'm saying is that on the practical side, on the subject of my everyday life, you have been a considerable help to me. You've been with me through some bad times. You've prevented me from doing some wild and foolish things. Obviously I haven't been coming here three times a week for two years for no reason. But all that doesn't mean that this article is something I can just forget.[7]

We may suppose that the author of *Portnoy's Complaint*, like Tarnopol, accepted the tragic conception of relations implied by the classical idea of transference. But not without qualifications. The things patients yearn for, love and dignity among them, have origins in families, but this does not mean they cannot also be absolute and mysterious. Should we not resist any analyst who reveals a bias against valuing as an end-in-itself the transcendent bond between parents and children? Sure, the bond may be deconstructed. But can you dismiss the impulse to devotion as a mere step and still really know what makes human beings (and even the writers among them) click?

"One of the things that was curious about Kleinschmidt as an analyst was that he was anti-children," Gopnik told me. He believed that the hope to gain any therapeutic benefit through fathering was a classic American illusion. It kept you from *the reality*. When I turned from therapy to parenting—I wrote about this in *Through the Children's Gate*—he was very disapproving. He thought it was, in plain English, a kind of sentimental, displaced narcissism. This was an oddity of his therapy. He was not one to encourage the notion that one could solve, or more precisely integrate what you learned about your own problems—that you can *transcend* those problems, in part, by doing a good job with your own kids, that is by having kids and making them central to your life. This was not something he had any patience for."

"Leaving Kleinschmidt became my ironic farewell to being a young guy, with the young guy's problems and self-attention," Gopnik recalls, "which meant finally seeing that the one solution he offered was to become more like him: a more patriarchal figure however comically or inadequately I would assume the role. For me, the one sane way out of the rat trap, out of the maze, was to say 'I can't resolve the things that happened to me before but

I can have kids and take on an adult role.' This was the door you went through, it was the way out. We had a two-month-old child, and we ran away to Paris, which he thought was a terrible idea, completely misconceived. Maybe it was, except I'm sure it wasn't."

And so a final point about *Portnoy's Complaint*, which I only implied earlier. Portnoy does not "solve his problems" or attain to anything like stability. Yet *Portnoy's Complaint* is an extraordinarily loving book. It is famously associated with the celebration of cockiness. But every page of *Portnoy's Complaint* is actually about the myriad pains of affection, for mother, father, sister, lover—which can make an artist—how did Gopnik put it?—"vulnerable."

Roth's power as a writer has always been in the off-handed, deeply *un*cynical ways he's implied such attachments to be the meaning of our lives—implied how our sense of sinfulness comes largely from the ways our loves come into contradiction. Our worlds go wrong, not because of selfishness, but because of sincerity. We get our relations wrong, and wrong again—and wrong *again!*—but this does not mean loving is vain or, worse, nothing but self-seeking projection. The last thing you can say about Portnoy is that, in his fierce autonomy, he aims to preserve a cold detachment at the center, though Spielvogel might well wish him this. Is it really just the artist who's motivated by hope for "the perfect communication of feeling," and is this really so pathetic? (Once, when I was experiencing a particularly difficult time, Roth told me: "Now your job is to *feel*.")

Nor am I revealing something readers of *Portnoy's Complaint*—but also *Patrimony, The Plot Against America*, and other works—do not already know when I say that Roth was a devoted son to his parents. As we read, fictionalized, in *Everyman*, some of Roth's most productive conversations have been at his parents' graveside in the Newark cemetery. *Portnoy's Complaint*, too, is ultimately about the natural gravity exerted by parents on children and vice versa. Children are a kind of Copernican revolution: the embodiment of what pulls you out of the center of things.

"I don't mean to imply," Gopnik concluded wistfully, "that I have figured things out. God knows, I haven't figured out anything. But trying however inadequately to play the part of a father is genuinely humbling. You become acutely aware of how *absolutely* inadequate you are— acutely aware of how it's *not your drama*. You go from being a boat to a port. I mean you stop being a person in the world whose fate is utterly consuming and fascinating, and you become Portnoy's father—the comic relief in the background of somebody else's life."

Once, back in 1985, when I had just published my own

first book, an older friend, a Polish Jewish writer and colleague at MIT, congratulated me, saying: "You must feel like you have just given birth to a child." "No," I said. "I am a father of three and this feels different." "Yes," she said, "you are right; children get bigger, books get smaller." I called Roth and told him. He really liked that line.

Conclusion
You Are Not True

Epistemology

I
Kick at the rock, Sam Johnson, break your bones:
But cloudy, cloudy is the stuff of stones.

II
We milk the cow of the world, and as we do
We whisper in her ear, "You are not true."
—RICHARD WILBUR

Portnoy's Complaint left us laughing and queasy and talking. Can you really *say* this? Is this also *me?* Was the doctor *really* right? The joke was on everybody—parents, lovers, tribes, patients, psychoanalysts—which is another way of saying it was on the act of reading itself. The novel's specific targets felt the impact most immediately:

mothers flinched, Jews howled, psychiatrists sighed. The most subversive thing about the novel was the subtle way it stepped on its own punch line.

Portnoy's Complaint's enigmatic quality contributed to its success as "literature." But future generations—I dare say, and will be mocked for saying—will read *Portnoy's Complaint* as a political or even philosophical document, a gloss on "emancipation," much like *Waiting for Godot* (also hilarious) is read. For Roth's early masterpiece burrowed under bourgeois liberty in a corresponding way, an epistemological way, and like *Godot* invited a reassessment of its foundations. Perhaps you cannot read *Portnoy's Complaint* twice. But you can't read it once without thinking twice about thinking. That (as President Obama shrewdly implied) is the novel's most lasting triumph.

Portnoy's Complaint did not simply undermine our sense of what happiness is or might be—by transgressing bourgeois norms, underlining ambivalent notions of sexual respectability, and so forth. It undermined the hope to *pursue* it with confidence in our language and perceptions. Roth did with Portnoy what Beckett did with Vladimir and Estragon, but his stage was not so bare or his dialogue so metaphysical. We did not have to be a sophisticated, battered European intelligentsia to savor the existentialism. We were urbane American liberals with our guard down.

Liberalism means, if anything, a commitment to a society of choices. But choose how and for what? This is no real problem for pundits on "roundtables" of Sunday morning talk shows—people often confused with liberals, but actually what we used to call behaviorists, people accustomed to telling us that, in making choices, we are bundles of appetites and ambitions, our "preferences" deriving from "socialization," our social connections reflecting our "demographic," our happiness a function of getting what we want, now. Hobbes, arguably the father of this behaviorism, taught that we want what world experience requires us to want, and then we seek power after power, the "present means to some future apparent good," and a stable game in which to acquire it. In this view, getting along means consuming goods, manipulating others' expectations to get them, turning our lives into projects, so that the only important reality is appearance—what Cokie Roberts and Sam Donaldson can agree on as "the perception out there." Behaviorism, Hannah Arendt once wrote, is not true but it can win.

After Hobbes, classical liberalism presumed that choice was something more interesting (or just less creepy) than this. Locke and his successors settled on the idea that people were moved to perfect their lives in discriminating ways. ("The mind thinks in proportion to the matter it gets from experience to think about," Locke wrote in his *Essay Concerning Human Understanding*.)[1] Later, John Stuart Mill read and absorbed some of Kant and assumed a certain individual creativity in learning and knowing; he thought we learned also from the clash of ideas. But as we saw with Franklin, there had always been a reactionary cast to Enlightenment ideas—especially their imported American versions—a stubborn belief in objectivity, suggesting principles of action that could seem almost as restrictive and narrowly pragmatic as what Hobbes had proposed.

"It is proposed to you that you mount a horse," Voltaire muses in the *Philosophical Dictionary;* "you must absolutely make a choice, for it is quite clear that you either will go or that you will not go . . ."

Up to there it is demonstrated that the will is not free. You wish to mount the horse; why? The reason, an ignoramus will say, is because I wish it. This answer is idiotic, nothing happens or can happen without a reason, a cause; there is one therefore for your wish. What is it? the agreeable idea of going on horseback which presents itself in your brain, the dominant idea, the determinant idea. But, you will say, can I not resist an idea which dominates me? No, for what would be the cause of your resistance? None. By your will you can obey only an idea which will dominate you more.[2]

For Franklin, we reasoned ourselves to happiness pretty much with the same methods of inquiry by which we built bridges or deflected lightning. The key was to discover the life experiences that proved to be sources of "dominant" ideas. At our best, as citizens, we could understand nature, understand human nature, and engineer things accordingly ("Let all your things have their places; let each part of your business have its time").

Implied here, as in the "natural philosophy" of the day, was the presumption that one could count on another person seeing pretty much what one saw oneself when both looked at "the same thing." Our lives could become objects to work on because of objectivity. Happiness, the end state of a life's work, was possible because experience bends thought the way gravity bends light. Okay, we are not *just* the products of socialization, not *just* matter in motion, but we are pretty close to these things; facts impress themselves on minds like a television absorbs a signal or a back absorbs a lashing. Hobbes famously called perception "decayed sense" in *The Leviathan*. We may call a tree by different names in different languages. But the picture of the tree grasped by the mind is more or less uniform and universal. Materialism begins with the power of matter to enforce its dimensions on people: we think that we know because we know what we think is not all that original to us. Our thoughts reflect the emanations of a consistent world.

"Concerning the thoughts of man," Hobbes writes, "they are every one a *representation* or *appearance*, of some quality, or other accident of a body without us, which is commonly called an object. Which object worketh on the eyes, ears, and other parts of man's body, and by diversity of working produceth diversity of appearances . . . for there is no conception in a man's mind which hath not at first, totally or by parts, been begotten upon the organs of sense." Locke added: "the mind has great power in varying and multiplying the objects of its thoughts, infinitely beyond what sensation or reflection furnished it with: but all this still confined to those simple ideas which it received from those two sources, and which are the ultimate materials of all its compositions."

Translation: Reality bites.

The satiric achievement of *Portnoy's Complaint* cannot be fully relished unless we understand how shrewdly, and with what alliances, it stood down these claims. Once it dawns on us that Spielvogel, too, is no privileged observer, the society of choices seems to us even more disquieting than what Portnoy had imagined. John Stuart Mill supposed that we enjoy liberty to sharpen our arguments and contribute our "piece of the truth." Could liberals find their footing if the truth was not a puzzle of pieces but a collage of patches? This was hardly a question for fiction alone. If the classical aim of the physical sciences was to give an exact picture of the material world, then a major achievement of physics in the twentieth century, as Jacob Bronowski beautifully put it, "was to prove that this aim is unattainable."[3]

It seems worth recalling that *Portnoy's Complaint* splashed powerful intellectual conventions at the time of its publication, especially in our burgeoning universities, where behaviorism was all the rage in social science departments. I cannot do justice here to the suffocating universe my friends and I confronted at the time, with syllabuses pushing books like *Quantitative International Politics*, or lectures about how—with the right "methodology," and powerful enough computers—every political event from elections to wars would be "predictable." The implicit message was that people were to be rendered in the old materialist sense. Our minds absorbed facts: facts economists told us about markets, facts that the RAND Corporation told us about states, facts that B. F. Skinner told us about happiness. To dissent, we were assured, was to posit mere "values."

Yes, the sixties were also a time of civil rights, mobilizations to end the Vietnam war, the New Left's discovery of the young Marx, and so forth. But what's persisted from the sixties, if only as an underground rebellion, and in no small measure thanks to writers like Roth, is an active resentment for the positivism that dominated the social sciences back then—a style of thinking that made political cynicism seem professional and politicians like Nixon natural. (Roth followed up *Portnoy's Complaint* with *Our Gang*, remember, a now-forgotten parody of the political language of the time: "With all due respect," so President Trick E. Dixon addresses his pastor, "we happen now to be listening to a man whose *business* is politics, just the way yours is religion, and if he says that in a situation like this one the truth and the dog and so on are not going to get us anywhere, then I must assume he knows what he is talking about . . .")[4]

Portnoy's Complaint did not attack this discourse head on. On the contrary, the book's edge is sharpened by our hero accepting its norms. Portnoy is, if anything, afflicted by *how much* he expects to be happy in utterly conventional ways, if not without some mischief; and Spielvogel's orthodoxy is not a dissent from positivism but a last-ditch effort to save it. With Spielvogel, as with Hobbes, freedom entails the recognition of necessity. Self-absorption is a fact before it is an unalienable right with constitutional protections ("So what's the crime? Sexual freedom? In this day and age?"). And by the amazing grace of the invisible hand, selfishness benefits all. Okay, insistence on lust is not a great theory of moral sentiments. The Playboy Mansion is not Monticello. But one way or another, your life is your project. What's required is a *science* of choices.

Portnoy's Complaint was hardly the first fiction to show how you could screw things up: build badly, hunger wildly, perceive dimly. You want a job you don't hate, a wife you don't hate, a home you don't hate. And by the time the novel came along, few educated Americans doubted that Freud was right, at least about things the Founding Fathers did not feel they could write into the Declaration of Independence: that all men are created equal, but with a little porn clip running in the back of our minds, which can turn life, liberty, et cetera, into a rough ride. (To save my grandchildren any embarrassment, I won't comment on the age the clip flips off; then again, Freud was also right about the tender age it flips on, and the decreasingly cute fanaticism, religious and political, that results from pretending it is not there.)

But the novel took things another step. Its satire corroded our confidence in knowing the very conditions that make us self-absorbed—not just the power of our erotic needs, but the unpredictable energy of wit, the limitations of perception, the fictionalization of everything. When

Roth said he had "done his part for fiction" he was, in part, a Prospero lamenting the imminent extinction of his magic. But he was also implying that inventing stories about one another is the best we can *ever* do, even in our everyday experience. Writers—the people who *consciously* invent people—are the closest thing we have to self-conscious beings, and their best inventions are the closest thing we have to the truth. "That's why you think you know Emma Bovary better than any woman you'll ever know," Roth told me. His *Portnoy's Complaint* demonstrated the point, deliciously, in a multi-layered satire Americans could digest, not entirely aware of what was happening, with mocking and peep-holes and pathetic claims.

"Roth has been the great stealth postmodernist of American letters, able to have his cake and eat it without any evidence of crumbs," James Wood writes perceptively in the *New Yorker*. "This is because he does not regard himself as a postmodernist. He is intensely interested in fabrication, in the performance of the self, in the reality that we make up in order to live; but his fiction examines this 'without sacrificing the factuality of time and place to surreal fakery or magic-realist gimmickry,' as Zuckerman approvingly says of Lonoff's work." Roth does not want us to think his characters are *just* characters, because (Wood might have added) the struggle is to render "character."

He does not call attention to what he is doing. Yet "he swims through depthless skepticism toward a series of questions that are gravely metaphysical. . . . How much of any self is pure invention? Isn't such invention as real to us as reality? . . . In this kind of work, the reader and the writer do something similar—they are both creating real fictions." *Portnoy's Complaint* was foundational in this sense. No straight thing is produced from its crooked timber, yet it left us feeling the shortest distance between points.[5]

As to the book's politics—and I shall be *pitied* for saying this—*Portnoy's Complaint* might well have been the real culmination of the civil rights struggle of the sixties, our awakening to liberalism's full implications. We were supposed to be judged not by the color of our skin but by the content of our character. The trailing insight of the book was that judging character was not going to be as easy as it sounded. The novel's readers discovered—thinking, and thinking again—that conscience, what Koestler once called the mysterious "first-person singular," must persist *without* empirical laws pointing to fixed, deducible ethical choices; that ethical explorations are inherently individual, subjective, limited by the senses, by lust, by interested experience, by vanity and trauma, time and place. The book undermined our fatuous belief in happiness. Yet it valorized what's proven to be liberalism's largest, most precious moral claim, that precisely because all perception is relative, the principle of tolerance must be absolute.

Nobody put this claim as sweetly, or directly, as little Ozzie in Roth's early story "Conversion of the Jews." "You should never hit anybody about God," he said, and *Portnoy's Complaint* leaves us with pretty much the same standard. Roth may demur, but I believe there is an apperception of the sacred here. We keep faith by building words and stories and pursuing a fugitive truth. In trying to penetrate another's character, we gain insight mainly into our limitations and another's inviolability. *Every human creature is constituted to be that profound secret and mystery to every other.* Still, we muster the courage to try something like understanding; we do our part for fiction; we fail. *Portnoy's Complaint* was a milestone in a life's work that demonstrated to Americans how little a "work" our lives are.

"I blew out the candle's scented flame," says the narrator at the end of *I Married a Communist*, visiting the elderly Uncle Murray, talking by starlight, "and stretched myself across the chaise on the deck and realized that listening in the black of a summer's night to a barely visible Murray had been something like listening to the bedroom radio when I was a kid ambitious to change the world by having all my untested convictions, masquerading as stories, broadcast nationwide. Murray, the radio: voices from the void controlling everything within, the convolutions of a story floating on air and into the ear so that the drama is perceived well behind the eyes, the cup that is the cranium a cup transformed into a limitless globe of a stage, containing fellow creatures whole. How deep our hearing goes! Think of all it means to *understand* from something that you simply hear. The godlikeness of having an ear! Is it not at least a *semi*divine phenomenon to be hurled into the innermost wrongness of human existence by virtue of nothing more than sitting in the dark, listening to what is said?"[6]

It is.

Notes

Prologue

1. Joe Peeples, "20th-Century American Bestsellers: *Portnoy's Complaint*," *Graduate School of Library and Information Science: The iSchool at Illinois* (http://www3.isrl.illinois.edu/~unsworth/courses/bestsellers/search.cgi?title=Portnoy's+Complaint).

2. "Librarians' Top 100 Novels of 20th Century," Nathan Jacobson, *Afterall.net* (http://afterall.net/books/490648); Richard Lacayo, "All Time 100 Novels: *Portnoy's Complaint* (1969), by Philip Roth," *Time*, October 16, 2005 (www.time.com/time/2005/100books/0,24459,portnoys_complaint,00.html).

3. Irving Howe, "Philip Roth Reconsidered," *Commentary*, December 1972.

4. *Philip Roth's Portnoy's Complaint*, Bloom's Modern Critical Interpretations (Philadelphia: Chelsea House, 2004), p. 2.

5. "Conversation: Philip Roth," *PBS NewsHour*, November 10, 2004 (www.pbs.org/newshour/bb/entertainment/july-dec04/roth_11-10.html).

CHAPTER 1. *A Novel in the Form of a Confession*

1. Peeples, "20th-Century American Bestsellers."
2. George John Searles, ed., *Conversations with Philip Roth* (Jackson: University of Mississippi Press, 1992), p. 38.
3. Lacayo, "All Time 100 Novels: *Portnoy's Complaint.*"
4. Google Books Ngram Viewer: *Portnoy's Complaint* (http://ngrams.googlelabs.com/graph?content=Portnoy's+Complaint&year_start=1800&year_end=2000&corpus=0&smoothing=3).
5. Alfred Kazin, "Up Against the Wall, Mama!" *New York Review of Books*, February 27, 1969 (www.nybooks.com/articles/11399).
6. *Alfred Kazin's Journals*, ed. Richard M. Cook (New Haven: Yale University Press, 2011), p. 390.
7. Todd Gitlin, *The Sixties*, revised edition (Bantam, 1993; originally published 1987), pp. 424–25.
8. Scott Raab, "Philip Roth Goes Home Again," *Esquire*, October 7, 2010 (http://www.esquire.com/features/philip-roth-interview-1010).
9. Andrea Chambers, "Philip Roth," *People*, December 19, 1983 (www.people.com/people/archive/article/0,,20086626,00.html).
10. Ibid.
11. Philip Roth, "Imagining Jews," *New York Review of Books*, October 3, 1974 (www.nybooks.com/issues/1974/oct/03).
12. "75 Years Since First Authorised American Ulysses," *The James Joyce Centre* (www.jamesjoyce.ie/detail.asp?ID=126).
13. Jan Pols, "The History of the Psychoanalytic Movement," *The Politics of Mental Illness: Myth and Power in the Work of Thomas S. Szasz* (www.janpols.net/Chapter-2/3.4.html).
14. David Remnick, "Into the Clear," *New Yorker*, May 8, 2000.
15. Philip Roth, *Reading Myself and Others* (New York: Farrar, Straus and Giroux, 1975), p. 142.

CHAPTER 2. *Really Icky*

1. Kazin, "Up Against the Wall."
2. *Alfred Kazin's Journals*, ed. Cook, p. 390.
3. "Superpowers," *This American Life*, 178, originally aired February 23, 2001.

4. D. H. Lawrence, *Studies in Classic American Literature* (New York: Penguin, 1977; originally published 1923), pp. 15, 18, 19.

5. Jodee Redmond, "Historical Divorce Rate Statistics," *Love To Know: Divorce*, LoveToKnow Corp. (http://divorce.lovetoknow .com/Historical_Divorce_Rate_Statistics).

6. Andrea Elliott, "The Jihadist Next Door," *New York Times Magazine*, January 27, 2010 (www.nytimes.com/2010/01/31/ magazine/31Jihadist-t.html?hp).

7. "Here," in *Begin Again: Collected Poems*, by Grace Paley (New York: Farrar, Straus and Giroux, 2000), p. 177.

CHAPTER 3. *"The Best Kind"*

1. Quoted in Gitlin, *The Sixties*, p. 172.

2. Irving Howe, *A Margin of Hope: An Intellectual Autobiography* (San Diego: Harcourt Brace Jovanovich, 1982), p. 252.

3. Sidra DeKoven Ezrahi, "State and Real Estate: Territoriality and the Modern Jewish Imagination," in *A New Jewry? America Since the Second World War*, ed. Peter Medding, Studies in Contemporary Jewry, vol. 8 (New York: Oxford University Press, 1992), p. 59.

4. Roth, *Reading Myself and Others*, p. 154.

5. Alan Cooper, *Philip Roth and the Jews* (Albany: State University of New York Press, 1996), pp. 110–11.

6. Diana Trilling, "The Uncomplaining Homosexuals," *Harper's*, August 1969.

7. Roth, *Reading Myself and Others*, p. 27.

8. Philip Roth, *The Professor of Desire*, reprinted in *Novels, 1973– 1977* (New York: Library of America, 2006), p. 808.

9. Philip Roth, *The Anatomy Lesson* (1983), reprinted in *Zuckerman Bound* (New York: Farrar, Straus and Giroux, 1985), p. 477.

10. Gerstein-Agne Strategic Communications, "National Survey of American Jews: March 2010," *J Street* (http://jstreet.org/new -poll-of-american-jews-views-israel/).

11. Ruth Wisse, review of *The Plot Against America* by Philip Roth, *Commentary*, December 2004.

12. David Biale, *Eros and the Jews* (Berkeley: University of California Press, 1997), p. 204.

13. Igor Webb, "Born Again," *Partisan Review*, October 23, 2000 (http://www.bu.edu/partisanreview/archive/2000/4/webb.html).

14. Philip Roth, *Operation Shylock: A Confession* (New York: Simon and Schuster, 1993), p. 312.

CHAPTER 4. *Punch Line*

1. "Internationale Zeitschrift Für (Ärtzliche) Psychoanalyse," from *Gale Dictionary of Psychoanalysis* (http://www.answers.com/topic/internationale-zeitschrift-f-r-rtzliche-psychoanalyse).

2. Philip Roth, *My Life as a Man*, reprinted in *Novels, 1973–1977* (New York: Library of America, 2006), p. 597.

3. Ibid., p. 599.

4. Ibid., p. 603.

5. Janet Malcolm, *Psychoanalysis: The Impossible Profession* (New York: Knopf, 1981), pp. 4–6.

6. Roth, *My Life as a Man*, p. 608.

7. Ibid., p. 604.

Conclusion

1. John Locke, *Essay Concerning Human Understanding*, Book II (http://oregonstate.edu/instruct/phl302/texts/locke/locke1/Book2a.html#Chapter II).

2. Voltaire, *The Philosophical Dictionary*, translated by H. I. Woolf (New York: Knopf, 1924), scanned by the Hanover College Department of History in 1995 (http://history.hanover.edu/texts/voltaire/volfrewi.html).

3. Jacob Bronowski, *The Ascent of Man* (Boston: Little, Brown, 1974), p. 353.

4. Philip Roth, *Our Gang*, reprinted in *Novels, 1967–1972* (New York: Library of America, 2005), p. 497.

5. James Wood, "Parade's End: The Many Lives of Nathan Zuckerman," *New Yorker*, October 15, 2007.

6. Philip Roth, *I Married a Communist* (Boston: Houghton Mifflin, 1998), p. 321.

Acknowledgments

My first (and best) reader is my wife, Sidra DeKoven Ezrahi. Some writers are able to put things lucidly almost from the start. I am not that writer, at least not when I am exploring a new argument. Outlines of chapters form in the head but they come out in a crush of claims, turns of phrase, and associations masquerading as sequential paragraphs. Sidra, bless her, is able to see the whole, enjoy the potential, and find words of encouragement—what she has done for her literature students at Hebrew University for forty years. And she seems to love me enough to read my many subsequent tries to untangle the strands and get out of my own way. Then she'll tell everybody about how good she thinks the result is. Oh, and that smile.

Philip Roth inspired the project with his genius and

supported it with his friendship. He sat for hours, helping me to test ideas, telling stories. To be clear, he did not endorse the result or interfere in any way with its composition. He is not that kind of friend, or writer. We have known one another well for many years, and I always thought of my book as a kind of tribute. Still, I undertook to write about *Portnoy's Complaint* with a certain neutrality and was not entirely surprised to find that its author could be even more impartial about its impact than I was. There was one small dispute, when I finally showed him a draft, and he felt my use of the recorded interviews was too extensive, his off-the-cuff words not polished enough, not meant for the page. "I don't want to be a character in your book," he said. I complied, reluctantly at first, but ultimately satisfied that the reason he wished words-in-quotes to be more or less effaced from my book proved its central point. Every construction is a fiction.

Jonathan Brent, the former editorial director of Yale University Press, suggested I do this book for the Icons of America series and waited patiently for the result. His successor, John Donatich, did the same and then gave the submitted draft the close, critical reading authors have learned not to expect from editors. My heartfelt thanks to both Jonathan and John—and to Phillip King, who combed through the manuscript with great care and professionalism. Early, post-Sidra drafts were read by my agent, James Rutman, and my friends Carlo Strenger, James Carroll, Alexandra Marshall, Nelson Aldrich, John Judis, Paul Bochner, Adam Gopnik, Igor Webb, and Christopher Lydon. All helped me in ways I cannot fully express my gratitude for here. Thanks also to other friends, Robert Alter, Daniel Boyarin, Hendrik Hertzberg, and Marianne Walters, for helpful interviews and expressions of support. Mike Emery, brand guru, the happiest goy in Herzliyah, read an early version of the introduction and suggested that the word "promiscuous" belonged in the title. That's why they pay him the big bucks. David Reisen taught me that psychoanalytic language heals when it does not purport to cure. This book would have been inconceivable had I not, with his compassion, searched out human nature in my story.

Thanks finally to my children, Ben, Ellie, and Tamar, who read drafts of the opening chapters and gave me reason to continue. It's nice when your children are old enough to know you the way you'd like to be remembered. The book is dedicated to Sidra's and my granddaughters, Maya Ezrahi-Kerr, Sofia and Jora Thompson-Avishai, and Lina Ezrahi, about whom words fail.

Index

happiness, 56–57, 116, 176, 200, 206, 209; humor in, 21, 42, 50–51, 54, 115, 125, 127, 143, 162, 180, 184, 199–200; and impotence, 13–14, 92–93, 116, 174; and Israel, 92–95, 103, 141–42, 144, 147, 159, 161, 175; and Jewish mother, 27, 49–50, 115–16, 119, 171–72; Jewishness in, 3, 4–5, 9, 13, 15, 22, 37, 49–50, 57, 60–61, 71, 91–92, 108, 113–14, 139–40, 149–50; lack of morbidity in, 84–87; and loyalties, 88–89; and marriage, 75–76, 88, 93–94, 119, 169; masturbation in, 2, 13, 14, 28–31, 36, 39, 40, 41, 48–49, 56, 59–64, 116, 162, 163–64, 169; and narrating Portnoy, 8, 9, 10, 13, 17, 18, 19, 29; and parents, 1–2, 13, 15, 30, 49–50, 53, 86, 87, 92, 99, 113, 114, 115, 125, 127, 128, 150, 161, 164, 168–69, 171, 180, 196–97, 199; popularity of, 3, 7–8, 14, 21, 25–26, 28, 37, 40, 41, 200; and Portnoy's self-effacement, 174; Portnoy's voice confused with Roth's, 19–20, 21, 35–40, 46–48, 51–56, 115, 123–24, 128;

as product of its time, 28–35, 36, 42–43, 56, 63, 83–84, 96–97; promiscuity in, 5, 20, 164; and readers' desire, 23; readers' memories of, 1–7, 62, 138–40; and the repellent, 80–81, 89, 137; reviews of, 26, 31, 35–36, 38, 59–60, 112–13, 115–27, 130; and stand-up comedy, 43–44, 45; and taboos, 26, 30, 32; and thinking, 43, 50, 55, 200; and tolerance, 210; women's reactions to, 81–83. *See also* Psychoanalysis; Satire
"Portrait of an Artist" (Roth), 45
Positivism, 126, 206
The Professor of Desire (Roth), 125
Psychoanalysis: as frame for *Portnoy's Complaint*, 14–16, 41–42, 45–50, 53–54, 56, 57, 73, 87, 94, 108; Howe on, 122, 127–28; and Kleinschmidt's article, 180–84, 189, 192–93; and narcissism, 16, 170, 176, 180–81, 183–84, 192–93, 195; Roth's psychoanalysis, 44, 177–80, 186–87, 192; satire of, 14–16, 22, 30, 40–41, 47, 61, 158, 159, 165–71, 176–77, 180,